The Game

Life vs the Dark Powers

by Gill Coombs

First published: 2016
Second edition: 2018
The author has given permission for this work to be freely shared
under Creative Commons principles
ISBN: 1539453359
ISBN-13: 978-1539453352

This book is dedicated to Life.

CONTENTS

GRATITUDE

My abundant gratitude to:

Peter Harrisson for his constant support, clear perception, and all the breakfast conversations.

Sarah and David McQueen for the use of Straw Angel Mill in the Auvergne: a truly inspiring space.

Mark Smart for helping me breathe this project to life. Matt Atkins, Jean Bolton, Howard Boorman, Stefan Cartwright, Lilith Flanagan, Steve and Sue Harrisson, Mandy Heard, Paula Hermes, Kathy Killinger, Will Knox, Mac Macartney, Sarah McQueen, Emilio Mula, Anne Newing, Paul Pizzala, Emily Reed, Tara Vaughan-Hughes, Biff Vernon, Nic Walker, Sarah Walker, and Andy Williamson for valuable discussions, in person and online.

Matt Atkins, Rajan Bowri, Terese Jaxmar Bruinen, Glenn Edney, Richard Elliott, Martin Griffith, Julie Holmes, Mac Macartney, David McQueen, Emily Reed, and Jan Young for commenting on various sections or drafts.

Trevor Eddolls, Jane Pares Edney, Giles Hutchins, Peter Harrisson, Anne Newing, and Malcolm Parlett, for their reading of the final manuscript and their valuable suggestions.

Artist/Hero Jo Stodgel for a captivating cover design and perceptive avatar illustrations; and Simon Watson for the author pic.

Deep gratitude to all those who consciously score for Life, no matter how much, or how often.

The Game: an Introduction

"All the world's a stage, and all the men and women merely players; they have their exits and their entrances, and one man in his time plays many parts." – William Shakespeare

Imagine two Forces: Life and The Dark Powers, engaged in perpetual action and counter-action.

In the Game, Life strives to create, evolve, and perfect itself through countless living forms. Its goals are survival, growth, and wellbeing. The Dark Powers control, constrict, harm and destroy that which is healthy and good, and threaten to obliterate Life itself. Their goals are wealth and prestige, and the control these make possible.

You're already playing the Game. This book shares information on how to play it in a way that's good for you, and for Life. It includes vital information that is not widely shared, and is sometimes even deliberately withheld. Life could lose the Game because so many people don't realise they're playing it.

In The Game, Life is pure creative energy in the form of every living being on the planet. The Dark Powers are not individual people, or even groups of individual people. They operate mostly under the surface, lurking in the shadows of four national and global establishments: Dark Media, Dark State, Dark Finance, and Dark Corporation. But the Dark Powers make use of real individuals to get what they want. They will make use of you if they can.

They do not particularly want the suffering and extinction of millions of species, emotional and physical harm to you, the players, or the shutting down of the planet's Life support system. That's just collateral damage in their quest for ever more power and wealth. There is no limit to how much power and wealth can be accumulated, as long as there is Life to plunder and dominate.

As a Player in the Game, you can score for either side every day. In fact, most things you do already score for one side or the other, even when you don't know it. This book contains basic but comprehensive information on how to score for Life, and how to stop the Dark Powers using you to score for them. The purpose is to lay out clearly what scores for each side, to help you to make informed choices.

The Game is played across twelve fields. In each field you have an avatar: the role you play. There are seven possible avatars: Manipulator, Cynic, Traditionalist, Sleepwalker, Avoider, Altruist and Hero. The avatars are also not individual people: they are like masks, worn temporarily. The actions you take in each field determine which avatar you are playing, and the points you score for either side.

Players move in and out of avatars. At any point in the Game, there's always a small number of Manipulator avatars manoeuvring for control, and Hero avatars trying to defend Life. Cynic avatars are out for themselves or carrying out the work of Manipulators, and Heroes are often supported in their work by Altruist avatars. A lot of players are in the Sleepwalker avatar, unaware that Heroes and Altruists are trying to defend them and all of Life from the Dark Powers. Traditionalist avatars are partly awake, but convinced the Dark Powers are doing the right thing. Players in the Avoider avatar are also partly awake: aware of the Game, but enmeshed by the Dark Powers into unwilling compliance.

When you don't know how to play the Game, you slip in and out of avatars without realising. But as you develop awareness, it gets easier to choose your own avatar. You have to be alert: your avatar will often morph without warning as you enter a new field, and it could morph within a field. And it's common to embody more than one avatar at a time.

You can play any of the avatars in any of the fields, but there will probably be one or two you usually play. You can learn to choose any avatar at any point in the Game, but not many players develop enough 'free will skill' to play consciously all the time. Most of us, no matter how experienced, get drawn into avatars without noticing. Some avatars might be harder to play because they're unfamiliar. Hint: the more you play them, the more natural they become.

You can influence (but not control) which avatars other players use. Players can disguise their avatars: they are not always what they appear to be. And of course players are often unaware that they are playing an avatar at all.

Both sides need players to score for them, but Life and the Dark Powers score in different ways. The Dark Powers use wealth to control: the more wealth they gain, the more powerful they are. As soon as you acquire a certain level of wealth you begin to score for the Dark Powers (there are exceptions to this rule, as you'll see later.) So Life has other tools for defending and evolving itself. They include awareness, courage, discipline and collaboration.

The first section of this book is your guide to the avatars. The information in these pages will help you identify at any point in the Game which avatar or avatars you are playing, which avatar you want to play, and how to do it. The second section gives a tour of the fields, and the way each avatar scores in each field.

Right now, the stakes are very high. The Game has been going on since time began, but is now accelerating rapidly into a new stage: every player can feel it. The future of Life as we know it now depends on the outcome. Losses to Life may put humanity out of the Game; it could even be Game Over for Life itself. When Life has no more to give, and there is no Life left to dominate, the Dark Powers have won. Otherwise, the Game goes on indefinitely.

This guide to the Game is not always an easy read - we are not living in easy times, as tension between the two forces heightens daily. But perhaps you're prepared to risk a little discomfort, at a time when Life is speaking directly to you: calling for you to do whatever you believe to be right, either in big ways or small. There is plenty of encouragement and inspiration here too.

So, are you in?

If you are: welcome. It's time to meet the avatars.

Hero

"Scared is what you're feeling. Brave is what you're doing." – Emma Donoghue

According to the dictionary, a Hero is 'someone who, in the face of danger and adversity or from a position of weakness, displays courage, bravery, or self-sacrifice for some greater good'.

It's a perfect description for the first avatar. When you're playing the Hero avatar, you're wide awake to the work of the Dark Powers, global or local. In this avatar, you have a strong conviction that it's your role to defend Life: to challenge the Dark Powers, and uphold all that is good.

To play Hero effectively, you make sure you're as well and accurately informed as possible. Then you stand up as tall as you can, and in your most powerful voice you challenge the Dark Powers: those destructive elements of the media, big business, the financial sector and the government, and dangerous random individuals. Speaking truth to power, you shatter the illusions that keep players spellbound and conforming to the norms the Dark Powers have created.

You challenge them verbally and directly, if you can get a platform. Or you make your voice heard through whatever channel you're most gifted in: creating online petitions, writing emails, blog posts, books, articles or poems; making films and sharing them on YouTube; creating subversive art; writing or singing powerful songs.

You fight vigorously for Life. You might organise and lead marches, peaceful protests, campaigns, or disruption to protest against that which is cruel and damaging: whether it's factory farming or austerity economics, loss of childhood freedom or climate change. You might give up your job and start up a business doing work that supports Life. Or, you score for Life through passive resistance: openly refusing to collude in what you believe to be wrong.

In the Game, Heroes make a visible difference to the scores; the balance of power. Think of Greenpeace, collectively embodying the Hero avatar as its trembling, passionate activists carry out acts of great daring to bring some great act of destruction to the world's attention. Whatever the damage: political power-grabs, habitat destruction, fracking, NHS sell-off – some Hero is on it. But they don't all make mainstream news. In Guatemala, indigenous activist Rigoberto Lima Choc was shot dead in 2015 outside a court that had earlier ordered a polluting palm oil factory to close. And in 2016 Berta Cáceres, who was campaigning about illegal logging in Honduras, was murdered in her home. You won't have heard about these Dark Corporation killings through mainstream media. But they continue to happen as indigenous peoples battle desperately to protect their ancestral lands. Heroism sometimes pays the ultimate personal price: it puts you out of the Game (even if your actions continue to score for Life long after you die).

Yet most of the world's daily Heroism isn't so high profile or dramatic. Think of the blogger who regularly calls out polluting companies, risking prosecution; the teacher who refuses to carry out shaming tests on young children, risking her professional status; the food factory employee who whistle-blows about dishonest labelling, risking his job; the child who challenges the Facebook bully or the adult who challenges the workplace bully, risking ostracisation. All are Heroes. In this Game, the Hero avatar is about finding courage when the situation demands it: taking risks to defend Life.

'Celebrity' Heroes include Emily Davison, who died in 1913 under the hooves of the King's racehorse, trying to draw attention to the oppression of women. Al Gore risked his political reputation to wake the world up to climate change with his eye-opening film *An Inconvenient Truth*. Pope Francis risked losing the respect of many wealthy and powerful supporters with his Encyclical (that should have been a Game-changing document, but somehow got forgotten by most). In it he asks whether it is realistic to hope that 'those who are obsessed with maximizing profits will stop to reflect on the environmental damage they will leave behind for future generations'. It was an open challenge to Manipulators, some of whom belong to his church.

You don't have to be perfect to play the Hero avatar. Prince Charles has long been speaking out for Life. He was faced first with ridicule, then criticism, and now charges of hypocrisy. He is justly criticised for his privilege and associated activities by Heroes working for equality. But his book *Harmony: A New Way of Looking at our World* shows his clear commitment to regularly playing the Hero avatar across several fields – though like anyone else, he sometimes plays other avatars too.

The role of Hero requires Courage: not necessarily fearlessness, but the ability to feel fear, or deep discomfort, and act anyway. Your Heroic acts will be judged, and you may well be publicly criticised. You suspect the cost of your actions may be high, but you have no way of knowing until you act. When you're openly standing up to Dark State, Media or Corporation, it's likely that you will be attacked: if not in person, then certainly online. You risk losing friends and alienating family, which is why the mutual support of collaboration between those defending Life is vital.

Courage can take surprising forms. Some Heroes were branded cowards in the world wars. They refused to fight, even though the penalties were severe – 'conscientious objectors' faced death, in many cases. Courage can be quiet; humble, even. An elderly Quaker, grateful for some small wealth, didn't mind paying tax on her savings: she saw it as a membership fee for belonging to society. But she passionately didn't want to contribute to the destruction that would be wrought by nuclear weapons. So she found out how much was due to be spent on nuclear arms in the coming year, worked out what percentage of public spending that represented, and then paid her taxes minus that. She was a financial conscientious objector. The bailiffs came and took her furniture, and she was threatened with prison. Eventually she stepped out of the Hero avatar. She had made her point.

When you're playing the Hero avatar you'll be called an idealist, as if that's a bad thing. But your idealism isn't naïve. In fact, the Hero avatar embodies more realistic hope, and is less deluded, than any other avatar. You'll be attacked for having principles. Some may reject the Hero as not being in the 'real' world, as if players were all powerless subjects of reality. However, reality is what all the players co-create – *that's what the Game is all about*. The Dark Powers, through players, make their contribution to reality through power, control and greed. Hero avatars counter them with idealism, vision and integrity.

Hero avatars make Dark State nervous, and you can bet it will try to suppress you if it notices your Hero activities gaining strength. If you've spent a lot of time in Hero, you're probably on Dark State's list. Your online activity is probably being monitored, and maybe your texts and calls, and possibly even your movements. But you're willing to take risks to defend what you love and believe in; to resist what you fear or despise. You're prepared to stand up for Life – even if you risk emotional, physical and mental wellbeing, self-esteem, reputation, livelihood, freedom, your physical safety or even your life.

However Courage alone isn't enough. It's no use having Courage, or acting bravely, without the wisdom to choose your actions well. That's like having a powerful engine, but no steering wheel. For example if you push your ideals too hard you may do more harm than good, triggering resentment. When you misjudge, the Dark Powers score. It can be a tough call, and collaboration can help, offering a sounding board.

Although it comes naturally to some, a lot of players don't *want* to play Hero. They would much rather be doing something peaceful, creative or fun. But these times call urgently for more Heroic work, and somehow players find the courage, time or energy to step up – at least for a while.

You can't play Hero all the time; no-one can. Engaging with the Dark Powers saps your energy and can burn you out. If you care enough to play Hero, chances are you're sensitive and could be overwhelmed by grappling with the sheer pace and volume of destruction in the world. Even experienced Heroes need a rest now and then – or occasionally feel the need to do something totally contrary to their values.

You may never choose the Hero avatar; it might not be your thing. And that's fine; you can still score for Life. Remember, you get to choose your avatar – as long as you're aware. But *any* Player can step up to the role of Hero, whether for a moment, a day, or on a regular basis, for as long as you're in the Game. Some players have just one go at playing Hero: a high profile, high energy time in their lives they'll never forget.

You may sometimes find the Game seems to choose the Hero avatar for you. The role that calls you – helping struggling refugees, standing for Parliament, or protesting about fracking – may take you regularly out of your comfort zone. But somehow, you keep finding courage and energy to draw on. You may experience a clear sense that your action is not only supported by Life, but *required* for successful completion of a certain stage of the Game.

Some players are so passionate about certain fields that they're prepared to accept collateral damage to Life defending what they believe in. Heroism can become extremism when religious fanatics and nationalists sanction mass murder; when animal and human rights campaigners send letter bombs. With the damage they inflict fighting for what they believe to be right, they're aiding the Dark Powers in their attempts to score for Life.

Sometimes the Hero avatar doesn't know its own strength; doesn't recognise its impact on others. An animal rights Hero might dedicate his life to freeing caged hens and pigs and wonder angrily why, no matter how hard he pushes, he doesn't get more support. He doesn't realise he has pushed people away, caused them to switch off. Maybe it doesn't occur to him that he hasn't supported other Heroes in their work.

All Hero avatars are in service of Life. It makes sense that each should operate primarily where they are most passionate and most effective. Collaboration and support might sometimes happen naturally, but expectations or demands don't tend to work.

You don't *have* to play any kind of Hero to defend Life from the Dark Powers. When your way of scoring for Life is less confrontational, you're playing the Altruist avatar.

Altruist

"The planet does not need more successful people. But it does desperately need more peacemakers, healers, restorers, storytellers, and lovers of every kind. It needs people who live well in their places. It needs people of moral courage willing to join the fight to make the world habitable and humane."

— David Orr

Altruism is 'the principle or practice of concern for the welfare of others'

   You're playing the Altruist avatar every time you act with the wellbeing of Life in mind, even when it's inconvenient. You're aware of health and wellbeing, suffering and injustice, in your community or beyond: whether your focus is society, economy, wildlife or climate. Playing this avatar, you take responsibility for your daily decisions. You play the Game consciously by acting for a happier and healthier world, maybe with particular attention to the field you care about most.

   You play the Altruist avatar every time you shop ethically, eat ethically; build community, support your local economy; contribute to ethical ventures and charities with money, skills or time; do work that benefits Life in some way; sign petitions and write to MPs, keep your carbon footprint low, keep the world free of rubbish and pollution; spontaneously help people or other creatures; encourage others who want to score for Life — and much more besides, as we'll see in the fields. You also consciously avoid activities that do direct or indirect harm to people, other creatures or the living world.

You don't necessarily need time or money to score for Life. But you do need those four tools: awareness, courage, discipline, and collaboration.

Awareness is vital: you need your eyes wide open to stay on top of what the Dark Powers are doing, and to avoid being manipulated into scoring for them without knowing.

The courage needed to play Altruist is a different sort than Heroic risk-taking. It's the courage to change behaviours, risk being thought eccentric, maybe give up some comforts. The idea of 'acting ethically' may make you nervous, although you don't know it until you seriously contemplate playing Altruist (and imagine telling your friends). If you feel a shudder of discomfort, a squirm of embarrassment about living ethically – that'll be coming from fear of something (a fear instilled by the Dark Powers). You'll need a good dose of courage, and collaboration can help you feel you belong, and are supported: a shared aim works wonders.

It can take discipline to live in a way that does no harm, especially if you relish pleasure, comfort and convenience. Sometimes the Altruist avatar has to make tough choices. However, it's not all sacrifice! Many find to their surprise that playing the Altruist avatar, once it's become habit, is enjoyable in unexpected ways. (Your pleasure scores bonus points!)

When you truly love something you don't want to harm it, and don't want others to harm it. Tending to the needs of Life comes naturally; in whatever way you do it best, for whatever you love most. When you do something good in the world, it can lead to a deeper fulfilment than any amount of money will give you. Plenty of Altruist avatars are busy creating the more beautiful world they know is possible; being the change they want to see.

To get right into the Altruist avatar, it helps to be somewhat in love with other players, with other living beings, with the world – and with yourself. There's no requirement for self-sacrifice or martyrdom in this avatar. How can you act on behalf of Life without attending lovingly to your own needs? If you are physically or emotionally broken? The Life within you needs you to address your own health and happiness first, and you're playing Altruist when you learn (sometimes slowly) to do this gladly.

Those defending Life have their strength not only in numbers, but also in collaboration. You can greatly improve on your individual score by joining with other Altruists: ten Altruists working together are generally more effective than ten working individually. The whole is more than the sum of its parts.

Playing the collective Altruist avatar, you aid Life in many ways. You share knowledge about the latest moves of the Dark Powers. You offer ideas about how to live in ways that are beneficial to Life rather than harmful. You use networks to pass on information about Life-enhancing products, projects and processes; recipes, tools and ideas; suppliers, experts, collaborators. Or you provide emotional support, information and encouragement to anyone feeling overwhelmed by the Dark Powers.

Alongside the work of Heroes, this collaboration of Altruists is Life's greatest hope. The Dark Powers do work together, but their relationships are driven ultimately by personal gain. This makes their alliances weaker and less stable – witness backstabbing politicians.

And yet, the cunning Dark Powers currently look like winning the Game. They've managed to make the Altruist avatar uncool, actively encouraging a culture of selfishness and mistrust. Dark Corporation makes *people* into *consumers*. Dark State makes it the norm to look after yourself and cover your back – minimising trust, empathy, collaboration, and reciprocity (essential ingredients for a thriving society). Dark Media goads players into spite, negativity and fear. And Dark Finance funds the others, whilst making it normal to put profit above people and planet.

Cultural acceptance of such a bleak 'norm' has led to a habit of embarrassment about playing the Altruist avatar: it's become almost shameful to be generous or kind. Maybe you score for Life secretly, or dismiss it by insisting you're not perfect, listing your flaws. Or you confess that your actions have some benefit, psychological or otherwise, to you.

You know what? If your ethical acts benefit you too, that's fine. In fact, we've already said there are bonus points: Life is all about wellbeing. Inhabit the Altruist avatar with pride: don't be ashamed that you've done something positive, and that doing it made you happy. When players are ashamed of doing good, good becomes marginal and secretive rather than normal and open, and bonus points go to the Dark Powers.

But let's be clear: the Altruist avatar doesn't represent perfection any more than Hero does. This avatar can be naïve or over-optimistic, sometimes trusting so much in Life that as you pass through the various fields wearing this Avatar you don't see the tricky bits coming: the snares and landmines laid by the Dark Powers. (Sometimes a dose of Cynic can be healthy – even vital.) Or you might indulge in pseudo-spirituality, placing trust in 'Higher Powers' and avoiding personal responsibility. In this Game, the Higher Power is Life itself, and that includes you.

Remember, it's possible to occupy two avatars simultaneously. For example, you might play Altruist in your concern for the environment, but simultaneously play Cynic about humans – hating our species for its destructiveness, missing out on the more beautiful aspects of humanity such as unconditional love and spontaneous kindness.

Alternatively, you might focus solely on humanity. This is natural: it's the species you belong to. But ignoring the wellbeing of other species and the living world, you're supporting the work of the Dark Powers. All Life is connected.

When you're playing Altruist, you don't criticise or judge those with different values or priorities: those playing Altruist only not like you do, or those playing other avatars. You might explain your view, but you don't give them a hard time as that generally scores for the Dark Powers. Anyway, you know only too well that no-one is totally perfect – as no-one is totally flawed. We *need* difference (as long as it's handled well). In diversity is resilience.

In this Game, there's no shame at all in playing the Altruist avatar partially or temporarily. But the more often you can play it (or even Hero) the better: all points scored for Life are welcome and much needed. Playing the Altruist avatar once in a while is so much better than never playing it at all.

You might be a habitual Altruist who needs to 'rest' sometimes. You know that at times you're not scoring for Life, or are even scoring for the Dark Powers. But you're kind to yourself: overall, you're doing the best you can. If you feel guilty and give yourself a hard time for not being perfect, you're probably playing Avoider.

Avoider

"The more you can escape from how horrible things really are, the less it's going to bother you... and then, the worse things get."

– Frank Zappa

To avoid is to withdraw; to look the other way. This avatar avoids responsibility, or cannot find any 'response-ability'.

When you're playing the Avoider avatar, you have awareness: you know all about the problems the world faces, and that you're sometimes complicit – but you lack the courage, discipline, or maybe the collaborators to do things differently. You know you're playing Avoider when you say 'I should be…' or have a vague intention of changing how you live… some time in the future. You know you're in Avoider when a desire to be (or be *seen as*) comfortably off, or to fit social norms, overrides your instinct to resist the creep of the Dark Powers.

Players sometimes slip into Avoider from Hero or Altruist, through a temporary shortage of courage, discipline or fellow collaborators. Sometimes you might suffer from overwhelm: there are so many heart-breaking petitions to sign, it's easier not to look at any.

Or perhaps, like many, you have been in the Sleepwalker avatar for a long, long time, and have begun to open your eyes. You wake up

16

and look around, only to realise that the world is heading for hell in a handcart. The knowledge is so appalling, you block it out of awareness. You quickly scroll past images that might cause distress; hide Facebook friends whose posts remind you of the dark side of the Game.

If you play this avatar often, you may have a well-practised habit of avoiding conflict or discomfort. Resolutely closing your eyes, you look away from disturbing images of exhausted refugees, child slaves making mobile phones, pigs cramped and bullied in an intensive farming unit. It may seem like you've done a good job of shutting that dreadful knowledge out. But you haven't shut it out. You've shut it in. Never again can you say, 'I didn't know'.

Consciously or otherwise, you know the world's leaders aren't taking care of you or your planet home. But despite your growing unease, you still don't vote for those who care about the world and its children. You agonise for a while, but end up voting for those who seem to promise a better economic future. You're not really surprised when pre-election promises are broken: at some level, you *knew*.

Despite your disappointment with politicians, maybe you don't – or can't – believe you could really take responsibility for yourself, your loved ones, and the future of Life itself into your own hands. In Avoider, it seems easier to let things happen to you and around you, even if you don't like what's happening. You feel the paralysis of overwhelm. You feel you couldn't possibly influence what happens in the world, or be any sort of leader! Making a difference might be off your radar, or even something you recoil from. The Dark Powers' grip on Life seems so complete, so inevitable, you don't know what you'd do anyway. You wouldn't know where to start.

The Avoider avatar is doing its best to protect its player. After all, you might struggle to find the Courage to walk away from a situation that's making you unhappy, never mind change the world.

But with courage and collaboration, you could make a real difference to the outcome of the Game. And you could feel much better for it, with a new sense of clarity, purpose, energy and self-respect.

Maybe you sometimes wonder whether scoring for Life is becoming the new norm. You know people who regularly play Hero or Altruist, but they belong to an alien world of 'ethical minorities'. It's like a different tribe. But you're increasingly noticing people like you talking about climate change as if it's real, caring about Syrian families, or buying free-range chicken. Perhaps you're becoming increasingly Altruist-curious…

A common misconception is that playing Altruist means living frugally. In the Avoider avatar, you might not want to change the way you live because of your desire to 'have nice things'. That desire might come from a sense of entitlement: you've always had nice things. Or maybe you had so little as a child that now you've finally got nice things, you're reluctant to give up your long-dreamed-of comfortable life. The good news is: you can actually live very comfortably and score for Life at the same time.

Of course, there's nothing 'wrong' in wanting or having nice things. Life is about happiness, and there can be much pleasure in objects that are beautiful, or useful, or both. The problem comes when those objects are made in great quantities: when they cause suffering to exploited workers, or are made using fossil fuel energy, or whole species meet the finality of extinction because the production of 'goods' means the clear-felling of the forest that is their home.

You can find out how the thing you want has been made – and where to buy (or how to make) an ethical version of it. There's an ethical version of just about everything you own (though some are more ethical than others). But when you're in Avoider, you can't summon up the energy to do the research. And it's not always just apathy. Maybe you suspect you'll find a trail of exploitation or destruction, and that would mean finding the courage or discipline to change your habits – either that, or feel guilty.

Speaking of guilt: perhaps you go into Avoider worrying that your sister in Hong Kong will complain if you stop flying; what your neighbour will say if you garden 'untidily' for wildlife; or what colleagues will think if you refuse daily sugary, fatty, well-meaning doughnut comforters. These are real fears: it's the most natural thing in the world to want to fit in; to be accepted. No wonder you get irritated, or downright angry, with do-gooders who make you feel guilty and stirred up inside (although those players you might think are sickeningly perfect are, of course, nothing of the sort).

In the Avoider avatar you may be too afraid *not* to ally yourself with the dominant ones, just as you may have been in the playground. You see and feel the strength of the Dark Powers in those around you. Even if you don't agree with what they're doing, you fear the shame and vulnerability of joining the minority.

Dark Media understands your fear. So they rubbish Altruist and Hero avatars, reinforcing the message that you're best avoiding them. You're secretly glad there are people fighting for Life; people living in a way that does no harm. You just don't want to be seen with them. But you're watching: sensitive to what could be a turning of the tide.

In Avoider there's often subconscious conflict between guilt over not acting for Life, and fear of doing so. To feel better you might go shopping, get drunk, get a takeaway, laugh with your friends about how much you've drunk, eaten and spent, take selfies; kidding yourself and each other that you think it's funny, when your body and soul (and maybe your children) know that it's really not.

If suppressed, this conflict might find its way out in irrational anger, or through comfort-eating or other mild (or more serious) addictions, poor sleep, or physical stress symptoms. Or it becomes buried under depression. Stress and depression are usually indicators that something needs to shift – and that the shift needs to start within you.

In Stephen Donaldson's fantasy novels *The Chronicles of Thomas Covenant*, Covenant is a kind of antihero. He is transported to a Land whose people believe him to be a character from ancient legend. He is convinced the Land is a delusion; a product of his disturbed mind. He could accept the respect of those he meets (and his responsibility to save the Land from corruption) but that would be dangerous.

If he were to relax and believe, he might be seduced by the beauty and innate health of the world he finds himself inhabiting, only to find none of it is real – which would be unbearable. So he refuses ever more desperate pleas for help so he can stay sane and grounded, keeping himself alive as others suffer and die. Ironically, in refusing to believe that a healthy Land and a beautiful way of living are possible, in denying the needs of the Land, he ensures his own death. Covenant was playing the Avoider avatar – and he knew it.

Avoider isn't an easy avatar to play. One way out of it is to make life easier by not giving yourself a hard time for something you're not willing or ready to change. Truly: why make things worse for yourself? When you suffer from your own guilt-tripping, that helps no-one – least of all you. It scores for the Dark Powers. The first step out of Avoider is to be kind to yourself, for however long it takes.

With increased awareness of the Game, you might find the courage or discipline to play the Altruist avatar sometimes. Having accepted the appalling reality of destruction, you begin to wiggle a finger; to free yourself from the paralysis of the Avoider avatar. Awareness, courage and discipline all need exercise. And exercise begins gently, with small steps, and collaboration.

Deep in Avoider, you may have buried your intuitive knowledge so deep, so safe, that you've lost sight of it almost completely. But if you truly have no idea about the consequences of your daily choices… you're Sleepwalking.

Sleepwalker

"*The general population doesn't know what's happening,*
and it doesn't even know that it doesn't know."
– Noam Chomsky

'Sleepwalking' is when you look as if you're awake but you're asleep, or in a sleep-like state. By definition, you don't know when you're in the Sleepwalker avatar. You're unaware of the consequences of your actions. The last few decades created whole generations made up largely of Sleepwalkers, and it's worth looking at how that happened.

The Dark Powers have always made use of Sleepwalkers. But as the UK recovered from the Second World War, Manipulators had increasing ability to communicate *en masse* to the whole country. Media had been used effectively to boost morale. People trusted what they heard on the radio, saw on television and read in the papers. The Dark Powers were watching, and sensed opportunities. People believed in the BBC, responded to adverts, and trusted familiar brands (then called 'makes'). Women were taught to be ideal housewives, and men encouraged to enter a job for life in industry or for the state. A sense of normality prevailed. This was comforting for those who had experienced hardship during and after the war – and played right into the hands of the Dark Powers.

A lot of players simply fell asleep under their persuasive spell. But there were always Hero avatars working for Life, challenging the Dark Powers as they gathered pace and created new forms of destruction: pesticides in the fifties, nuclear arms in the sixties, the rise of junk food in the seventies. Often isolated, those playing Hero were labelled radicals, weirdos, agitators, or lunatics. In the days before social media, it was harder to find like-minded others for support.

Players who were still awake realised what was happening, and some rebelled. In the sixties, hippies responded to the threat of war with love, and voiced concern about industrial degradation of the living planet. In the seventies, there were bikers. They saw players around them losing their wild selves, dipped in saccharine and corporate lies; they responded with heavy metal rage. Then there was punk, which fought back aggressively in its fury at being subdued and exploited by Dark State.

But during the eighties a generation of players were put back to sleep, both in the UK and elsewhere. Maybe you too were gently lulled by convenience and luxury, lured by easy credit, anaesthetised by commercial pop music, and deceived by a Dark vision of national success. Many were enchanted by a 'new wave' phase that encouraged them to develop a grandiose version of themselves: big hair, exaggerated body shapes, the artificial voices cloned by customer service staff taught to speak like robots.

Maybe you were encouraged by ads, magazine articles, and workplace competency frameworks to strive towards an aspirational norm. Maybe you hoped that luxury furniture on credit, wide screen TVs and designer toiletries would bring the sense of success you yearned for, even as they plunged you deeper into debt and emotional isolation. And in the decades since, the dumbing down of TV and increasing power of corporations have together tightened the Dark Powers' paralysing grip.

The Dark Powers know that when you feel alone or unhappy, you're more likely to consume. When you've been sucked into the Sleepwalker avatar you consume trustingly: food, information, services, or just 'stuff'. Your only questions are: do you like it, do you want it, is it past its sell-by date, is it a bargain, will it make you look good? You want to believe in a bottomless purse, an indestructible planet, and a Happy Ever After. When stories come on the news about war, drought, and refugees, you feel a stab of pity, perhaps followed by relief that you live in a safe and prosperous country.

Materially, life is comparatively easy if you're living in one of the world's wealthiest nations. Unless you're living in severe poverty by UK standards, basic needs like heat, light, and water are met at a touch. You can communicate with people all over the world, get in a car and drive where you like, walk into a supermarket and choose from endless shelves and chiller cabinets of produce from all over the world. You take these things for granted, and quite naturally… they've probably been available all your life.

Compare this with a tribe of people who have no choice but to make their own shelter, forage or kill everything they eat, light fires to keep warm. This is how your own ancestors lived for hundreds of thousands of years, and because they did it so successfully, you are sitting and reading this book right now. That long period of pre-history wasn't Utopia. Your ancestors knew fear: they knew it daily, and it kept them alive and alert (although without the cures we have today, their lives were short). They knew hunger, and it made them grateful for whatever food they could obtain. They knew hard work, and it kept them together through times of conflict, as they collaborated for pleasure or survival.

The Sleepwalker avatar is like a domestic dog compared to a wolf; a dairy cow compared to a wild bison: compliant and dumbed down rather than alert and responsive. Sleepwalking, you don't notice the threats and opportunities in a complex, ever-changing Game. You don't take truly mature responsibility for finding out what's going on in the world: you let the media do that. Luxuries and conveniences have left you unskilled in the raw act of living.

Responsibility for your wellbeing has shifted from you and your community to the state, and to corporations that happily sell you everything you need to live – and convince you that you need a *lot* more to

24

live than you actually do). Sleepwalker is the most childlike avatar: in this role you're happy to allow those parent-like figures to look after you. When you're playing Sleepwalker (which probably isn't all the time) you believe what you're told; buy what you're sold.

This loss of independence and self-sufficiency wouldn't be so dangerous if state, media, corporations, and banks were reliably good, benevolent parents. But while we slept, the Dark Powers were strengthening their occupation of each sector, growing ever more powerful. Those who saw and tried to challenge the growing force of the Dark Powers, to stop other players falling under their enchantment, were easily ridiculed and called eccentric by the Dark Powers. And Sleepwalking players just went along with it.

Mainstream education taught children to pass tests, but not to stay awake and aware; to think for themselves. The soundbites and the image-dominated information we're fed make our brains lazy. We're Sleepwalking when we forget how to research, question and decide for ourselves. You can imagine how this might develop: the Dark Powers' control becoming complete through carefully designed 'news', ever more subtle and pervasive marketing, the spiteful, divisive tone of the media, and seductive perks for employees. Imagine a passive, working, consuming society feeding the elite with their lives…

But then came the internet, and with it everything changed. The power of mass communication no longer lay only with powerful Manipulators. It lay increasingly with the players. As a result, more and more have been waking up to the Game. The political turmoil that began in 2016 was, for many, a shocking eye-opener to the machinations of Dark State. Most people now recognise the impending threat of climate change, which wouldn't have happened if the Dark Powers had complete control of communication. But even so, plenty are still Sleepwalking: believing the lies peddled by Dark State about why it subsidises fracking, gives tax breaks to the oil industry and cuts support for renewables.

Sleepwalking doesn't equal low intelligence. You might excel at maths, logic, remembering facts, problem-solving, organising or other skills – but have your eyes closed while grocery shopping, not seeing the connection between the destruction in the world and the contents of your shopping trolley.

And Sleepwalkers don't necessarily lack courage. Some very brave Sleepwalkers carry out substantial acts of destruction, because they don't get the impact of what they're doing. It happened during the world wars. It was replicated later in experiments where players were invited by 'authority figures' to give others electric shocks. But in the Sleepwalker avatar, we don't learn from history and recognise that it's happening again, now.

Sleepwalking doesn't exclude empathy. You might be loyal and caring to family, community or country. But beyond that, others' suffering doesn't seem quite real; maybe doesn't seem to matter very much, if you're honest. Your circle of concern might expand sometimes, when a hashtag like #AylanKurdi goes viral. Such a tragedy could wake you up permanently to the Game – or you could slide back into the Sleepwalker avatar.

Sleepwalking, you don't realise you're marching blindly but steadily towards the edge of a global precipice. You aren't aware of the efforts of Heroes to protect Life, including you, from the Dark Powers. Let's not forget, though: those players also sometimes wake up to find they've been Sleepwalking. Sometimes they're so busy playing Hero in one field, they score for the Dark Powers in others.

If you've been in the Sleepwalker avatar for a long time, you may find your eyes gradually opening to the Game as the edge of the precipice draws near. When this happens, you won't have to look far for other players ready and willing to collaborate. But if you know all the arguments and *still* don't want anything to change, you're playing the Traditionalist avatar.

Traditionalist

"Human beings have a great capacity for sticking to false beliefs with passion and tenacity." – Bruce Lipton

A traditionalist believes in and follows traditional ideas. The Traditionalist avatar upholds tradition *simply and precisely because it is tradition.*

When you're playing this avatar you're awake, but with blinkers on. Your focused view puts everything you encounter either in or out of the 'acceptable' box. You have firm opinions and allegiances: nothing's going to change your mind, and you're proud of it. When other players voice ideas very different from your own, you dismiss them confidently and immediately.

You can score for Life playing this avatar, when you bring family and community together for traditional activities that nourish body and soul, or when you fight persistently for something you cherish. You may be a decent person who plays Traditionalist passively, stubbornly refusing to open your mind to new ideas, whichever side they score for. But some play it viciously, deliberately sharing misinformation about anyone whose views they're opposed to: trolling, doxing and making personal attacks when they lack facts; stirring up hatred, encouraging violence. Naturally such behaviour scores for the Dark Powers – whatever they're attacking.

But the Traditionalist avatar is a keeper of the *status quo*, and generally provides important underpinning for society. Its strength of purpose is admirable, and the Traditionalist can be kind and generous. But tradition, as well as being culturally important, can also justify harmful activities and negate ethical objections. Playing Traditionalist, you might accept *foie gras*, knowing how it's made, because it's always been a status symbol in your circles. Or you approve of fox hunting because we've 'always' done it in this country; or you believe in God because – well, just because you do. None of these activities makes you 'a Traditionalist' on its own: you're playing this avatar when you believe they're right *because they've always been done*. (If you justify a damaging tradition simply because you enjoy it, with no thought of the broader consequences, you're playing Sleepwalker.)

Some players hold considered and sincere religious or spiritual beliefs and are some of the Game's great protagonists for Life. But Manipulators also run religions, and they want you to play the Traditionalist avatar. They actively discourage questioning, cleverly instilling the message that to doubt is sinful. You're not permitted to step outside your own faith to look at it objectively, or from other angles. This holds you in a fixed position of tunnel vision. You could stay in Traditionalist throughout the entire Game – unless something deeply personal and disruptive happens to send you lurching out of your rut.

The Traditionalist avatar appreciates authority, discipline, control, clarity, and a power hierarchy. These sound like adult, parental qualities and they all have their positive aspects. Yet there's something childish about the Traditionalist avatar, as there is with Sleepwalker. This avatar might be forceful in its expression, but it accepts authority without questioning, and so never grows.

Sometimes players *seem* awake, as they fight hard for what they believe in. But when you believe in something without being able to say why, or offer set reasons that don't stand up to deeper questioning, you're probably in Traditionalist. Some greater authority on what is Right (family tradition, the government, the Bible or the daily paper) carries more weight for you than carefully researched facts. This, of course, is very useful to the authority.

Players who stubbornly refuse to believe consistent scientific evidence about climate change are playing Traditionalist (those who thoughtlessly believe the lies strategically and expensively spread by the Dark Powers are Sleepwalking). For habitual Traditionalists, a forceful, entrenched position sometimes masks a fear that 'if I admit I'm not completely right, that would make me completely wrong, and that would be unbearable.'

Such a fear is often left over from childhood, when we saw everything in absolute terms, with no grey areas: if it's not this, then it must be that. When you find yourself in the Traditionalist avatar, something's triggered you to revert to that childish perspective, and you lose your adult understanding of complex situations. Climate change can't be caused by humans: if it is, the hippies were right, and you were wrong. And that's unthinkable.

Any players can go into Traditionalist when their most cherished beliefs are questioned. Maybe you abhor 'unnatural' inventions such as the internet, drones, or chainsaws. Perhaps you refuse to consider nuclear power, geo-engineering, or genome science. If you've done the research and come up with considered reasons, you might be in Altruist or Hero. But if technological advances just make you feel deeply uneasy, you could be playing Traditionalist without realising. What if the advance you fear is the one that could preserve biodiversity and help Life to thrive? Such dilemmas take us into fields that are tricky to navigate.

It's change that the Traditionalist avatar fears: the fundamental threat to what we have always known. If you protest, "But people have always done x", you're probably playing Traditionalist. People have existed for hundreds of thousands of years, and chances are you're defending something that only came on the scene in the last few generations. What you probably mean is "But I've always done that, and so did my parents, and maybe even their parents too."

When you're playing the Traditionalist avatar, books are only 'proper' if they're published by a publishing house; art is only art if it's hanging in a gallery. You consider nothing valid unless it's approved by the appropriate authority.

And maybe there's something else going on. You might have grown up in an environment that felt threatening and uncertain. Perhaps as a small, vulnerable child you found life terrifying. You may have protected yourself by creating a stable and structured understanding of the world, so if anything ever went wrong, you could put it neatly in the most appropriate box and deal with it. You skilfully created this safe world without knowing you were doing so. Its illusion of certainty is so complete, no wonder anything that rocks the boat is alarming and to be rejected. If everything you believed was turned upside down and stood on its head – imagine the frightening collapse of stability, and ensuing chaos. Naturally that feels like something to fear (though sometimes, the fear is worse than the reality).

Dark State knows all about your fear. It speaks of strength and stability, amplifying your aversion to change, reassuring you that it's taking the country in the right direction. In reality it's leading you into societal and environmental crises, in order to feed the increasingly powerful Dark Corporation and Dark Finance. Governments today have no clue how to shape an increasingly complex world they've lost control of. Meanwhile Dark Media alarms us with spiteful headlines, confirming and amplifying our fears and suspicions. Fearful players are far easier to control.

A reminder of the rules of the Game: if you believe a tradition has a sound ethical basis and involves no harm, then defending it scores points for Life. But if you hold out for a tradition detrimental to Life, you're scoring points for the Dark Powers. Some situations are complex (as you'll see shortly in the fields). But there's no higher authority that can tell you absolutely what is Right and what is Wrong in every situation. You're going to have to make your own moral and logical decisions if you want to score for Life.

It's worth considering that if enough players defend the wrong traditions, we will likely have rapid and horrible change foisted on us anyway, and find ourselves amidst the chaos and danger the Traditionalist avatar dreads. If we all defend the use of oil for driving and flying, the resulting climate chaos is going to be hugely disruptive. You may say, 'But driving is part of our lives; we have to have oil'. Really? Maybe it's time for a careful and discerning examination of those traditions – and the alternatives.

When you're in Traditionalist, you may feel that nothing is possible other than the familiar. But humans are amazingly adaptable and resilient. Humans have adapted many times, and will have to adapt many times more before the Game is over. Your beliefs, decisions and actions matter. They could make all the difference. During an extremely mild winter with floods of biblical proportions, some started to feel concerned. Normality felt threatened: "The weather's *not right*". Perhaps players in Traditionalist will become some of our greatest Heroes as they perceive the danger, and fight vigorously to defend what they believe in.

The Traditionalist avatar doesn't want change; it believes in the *status quo*. The Cynic, however, doesn't believe in much at all.

Cynic

*"A cynic knows the price of everything, and
the value of nothing." — Oscar Wilde*

If the Altruist avatar can be gullible, and the Traditionalist avatar has firm but ungrounded beliefs, then the Cynic avatar is founded in *dis*belief.

When you play Cynic, you're not inclined to believe anything or anyone without good reason. You know blind trust can get you screwed over, and the Cynic avatar protects you from that. But it can also be closed to ideas for making the world a better place, and suspicious of those who are genuinely well-intentioned. Holding back in the Cynic avatar, you miss out on the best bits of the Game – and Life misses out on everything you've got to offer. Somewhere between gullibility and suspicion there's a healthy position of questioning and evaluating: keeping an open, discerning mind.

You might think playing Cynic is neutral in terms of scoring. A dose of healthy mistrust can provide a good balance for well-meaning altruism, and the Cynic avatar can also save its Player from believing (like the Sleepwalker and Traditionalist) that all's well when it's really not.

But some players in Cynic are unwitting tools of the Dark Powers. Scorn for ethics in business or science, for example, plays into their hands: if we reject or ignore the importance of compassion, fairness or even happiness, that makes anything acceptable in the name of progress (or profit), no matter how destructive.

Also, you might actively score points for the Dark Powers in refusing to believe that your work, purchases or decisions could make a positive difference to the Game. The whole world situation looks so bleak, you might feel it's naïve to believe you could make a difference. When players wear the Cynic avatar, it gives the Dark Powers a significant advantage. When we think the Dark Powers are bound to win and don't bother trying to score for Life, it's a self-fulfilling prophecy. That's why the Dark Powers sell us such a bleak world-view, and it's ironic that Cynic avatars believe it.

In this avatar you may have an underlying sense that everything's going down the pan, and you're not surprised. Accustomed to disappointment, you've built a hard shell around your tenderness. You dare not believe in goodness: the possibility that Life could thrive, and diminish the grip of the Dark Powers.

When you're in this avatar, you view the world, and people's behaviour, through a cynical lens. You see the negative in people and situations, and maybe in yourself. Mistrustful of motives, you're unable to conceive that those playing Altruist and Hero are acting from genuine concern rather than self-interest.

Perhaps you fake gratitude when someone offers you help. But you're weighing up their motives: what do they want from you, and will it be worth it? Notions of simple generosity or compassion don't wash; you're not that naïve. The disappointed idealist in you might have believed in altruism, but bitter experience has taught you otherwise, and you won't get caught out again.

You're playing Cynic when your approach to community is based on personal gain, others' usefulness and a healthy mistrust. When others joyfully share an achievement, you interpret it as trying to get ahead. You pretend friendship to players who might be useful. If they fall for it and feel hurt when you no longer have use for them – they shouldn't have been so stupid.

The Cynic avatar acts from self-interest. If other players are out to screw you over, why not beat them to it?

This avatar scores for the Dark Powers not only by negating genuine good intention, but by sowing mistrust amongst other players and pulling them into the Cynic avatar. Expressions of kindness, courtesy and care become clichéd and debased: sincere language is cynically used, and loses its true meaning.

For a long time, when humans lived in small family groups, they'd have to trust each other to survive. Alongside the joy of strong relationships, they'd know everyone well enough to gauge when not to trust. But where communities have disappeared, most others we encounter are strangers. Once, strangers were usually cautiously welcomed, but today players generally go into Cynic, and start from a position of *mis*trust. That's inflamed by a culture that promotes a Cynical approach to work and relationships, driving a culture of competition and covering your back, rather than collaboration. You're so used to being manipulated by ads and spin, you've come to expect it from everyone. So you stay on your guard.

Even if you're a habitual Cynic, it's unlikely you were born that way. Comedian and author George Carlin said that inside every cynic is a disappointed idealist. Maybe Cynic is the avatar you adopt to protect yourself from the bitterness of a harsh world inhabited by flawed people.

You might believe Cynicism will keep you ahead in the Game. But that's a mistake. You might think you're winning when you're gaining at the expense of others. But in this Game, as inequality increases the Dark Powers get stronger. Divided, all players are more vulnerable. They're easier prey. Alternatively, when it looks like you're losing the Game compared to others, you might slip into Cynic and decide not to give a damn.

All players find themselves inhabiting the Cynic avatar sometimes. Your cynicism might be about people, establishments or ideologies – whether capitalism or communism, or qualities such as honesty, integrity, or altruism; emotion or intuition.

The Cynic avatar covers a spectrum from soft Cynic (similar to Traditionalist but better informed) to dangerously hard Cynic. Passive

Cynicism is often accompanied by a sense of helplessness. You're resigned to destruction, however bad it might be. *That's the real world.* Such despair is understandable, but dangerous. It helps no-one (least of all you), and allows the Dark Powers to make gains.

The hard Cynic, though, has a mercenary quality. You're playing this avatar if you're happy to gain personally, regardless of the destruction you cause. You're awake, and aware of suffering in the world. You don't know all the details, and you don't need to – not because you couldn't bear the pain (that's Avoider), but because you don't care. You're prepared to add to the world's suffering if you benefit. Beyond that, you're not interested.

When you play hard Cynic (and you may never play this avatar), you're generally in willing service of the Dark Powers – that's where the money is. But you can switch sides when it suits. A Player in Cynic can appear to be playing Hero or Altruist: if there's something in it for you, you'll teach on the sustainability programme, run the wind farm, support local businesses and so on. Perhaps you invest in renewable energy – not because you're worried about an acid ocean, but because share prices are high. But if you're not gaining, you'll pull out without any fuss and put your time and money elsewhere. If the oil industry benefits, or the programme collapses, or the local trader goes bankrupt – tough. And why not? You believe all the other players would do the same, given a chance.

If you play at the hard end of the Cynic avatar, you're playing close to the Manipulator avatar. Perhaps you're carrying out work for a Manipulator, sucked in by their promises of wealth and power in direct exchange for the damage you're prepared to cause on their behalf.

Manipulator

*"Darkness cannot drive out darkness; only light can do
that. Hate cannot drive out hate; only love can do that."*
– Martin Luther King

Most of us are manipulative with a small 'm' sometimes (often without
even knowing it). But that's different from playing the Manipulator avatar
in the Game.

There are probably only a few thousand players in the role of global
class Manipulator; we don't know for sure. You can only play this avatar if
you have a strategic overview of the whole Game, fake but utterly
convincing charm, and are even more ruthless than Hard Cynic. Most
Manipulators inhabit the four Dark Powers, although some operate
independently. Global Manipulators have colossal power, and pretty
much run the Game.

But plenty of players can and do access a smaller Manipulator avatar,
scoring for the Dark Powers as they gain in strength by undermining
others or causing them to be excluded.

The Manipulator avatar consciously engineers situations to get the
outcomes it wants – either for personal gain or intellectual entertainment.
Manipulator avatars know better than any that life is a Game, and have
various subtle and cunning strategies for winning. Psychologically adept,
they have an ability to read others, and influence their thinking and
behaviours without them realising. The Manipulator avatar is wide awake
to both the possibilities and implications of exploitation.

Those who regularly play this avatar probably began their career of Manipulation in the playground. At a tender age they might already have felt a fundamental sense of worthlessness, impotence or despair – and that made a sense of control extremely desirable. They swiftly worked out power structures, alliances and tensions so they could work them to their advantage. They used convincing but totally false charm to get others' loyalty. Perhaps they were the 'popular' child – not because they were the kindest, funniest or nicest to be around, but because they were charismatic; they held the power. Other kids were afraid of them, preferring an uneasy, insincere 'friendship' with them to the social death of exclusion. They tricked other kids into revealing embarrassing secrets, weaknesses and hidden fears so they could feel superior. Later they could hold that knowledge against other players; use it as currency. Manipulators avoid those who exude a sense of self-worth and integrity, knowing they won't play their Game.

Playing a minor Manipulator avatar you might use similar tactics today in the workplace, with family, and in your social circle. You've developed your skills, and your strategies have become more subtle. One Manipulator can spot another. Another Manipulator is either your deadly rival, or the closest you have to a true friend. Manipulators with bigger avatars may well notice you. If you dare to get involved with them, they will know just how to manipulate you through your gut fear of diminished power.

The global Manipulator is ambitious in its scope. The aim is to amass as much power, wealth or prestige as possible during one life. The ultimate goal is control. Unlike plain ambitious entrepreneurs, the Manipulator avatar is chillingly ruthless in its execution. It almost always involves exploitation or obliteration of fellow human beings, other species, habitats, or the whole planetary ecosystem. So the Manipulator avatar ultimately serves the Dark Powers (if you're a cunning Game-player using your coercive skills to serve Life – you're playing Hero).

Those playing a big Manipulator avatar exude power, and know it. Skilled in deflecting personal blame and legal action, often avoiding the public eye, they make use of others to carry out their dirty work. Hard Cynic avatars, which lack social responsibility but lust for status or money, are useful tools. Traditionalists, Sleepwalkers and Avoiders make good pawns if they can be kept working and spending. Manipulators use what they need to get what they want: blackmail, coercion, playing on fears, offering bribes, seduction, violence, or murder that can never be traced back to them.

Manipulator avatars aren't out to destroy the world. And yet that's exactly what they're achieving, as through them the Dark Powers create climate chaos, ocean acidification, mass extinction, deforestation, extreme poverty, war, and death. Why would extremely clever and strategic individuals cut off the very branch that we're all sitting on – including them?

An enlightening film about the global Manipulator avatar is *The Corporation*. It explores the move to grant giant international companies the same legal rights as humanity, asking: if businesses were humans, what kind of humans would they be? It concludes that the global Corporation, if it were a person, would be a psychopath: ruthless, egocentric, selfish, deceitful and irresponsible; considering themselves outside the law, and with no remorse. Of course not every chief exec or company chairman is a psychopath. Many do good work. But the biggest and most powerful corporations often become dispassionate giant machines that no-one feels they have control of any more, playing a collective psychopathic or sociopathic Manipulator avatar.

In a way, you can see why global Manipulators (whether operating as CEO, media mogul, senior politician, or big banker) wouldn't hesitate to saw off the branch the rest of us are sitting on, if they gained from it. These avatars are ruthless in their pursuit of personal gain for wealth, or the control and power that wealth brings. But they *are* sitting on the same branch, and they know it. Whatever else Manipulators are, they're not stupid. They can join up the dots in ways most players could never dream of. So why are they putting themselves, apparently deliberately, in such danger from environmental catastrophe?

Maybe world class Manipulators feel untouchable. Maybe they can't imagine a problem they can't buy themselves out of. If they accidentally trigger nuclear war, they'll have highly sophisticated bunkers to hide out in. If climate chaos worsens, they will command the last safe havens, the last liveable territories; gated communities of climate change denial. Such places will have expensive, ruthless security to deter climate refugees (who will be most of us).

The elite are already investing in elaborate structures able to support human life, at least in the short term. Some are buying up land in New Zealand, so they can take themselves as far away as possible from possible nuclear war in the northern hemisphere. And some are banking on getting off the planet before it's too late (though it's hard to imagine what any future for humanity might look like in that scenario).

Perhaps one reason for such self-destructive behaviour lies in the fact of the Game. Manipulators are more aware of the Game than any other avatar apart from Hero; it's what they live for. Moving pawns around, taking risks, winning and losing, forming dangerous alliances, making treacherous moves, wiping out other players; this is what the Game is about. As we witness the unravelling of our climate and our thin societal fabric, maybe some Manipulators get a thrill from the risk. How much power will they be able to amass before the Game ends? Will they be able to get the timing exactly right, and check out of the Game just before it's over?

It could be that like any gambler they know they're destroying themselves, but that's trumped by compulsive behaviour where power is concerned. There's no such thing as 'enough', or it's always just round the next corner: after the next hostile takeover, the next powerful alliance, the next seam of exploitation.

In this guide to the Game, global Manipulator avatars are usually referred to as 'them'. They are few in number, and it's unlikely any will be reading these words. But if you are one of the ruthless individuals who knows full well that your actions are destroying people, creatures and biosphere: one way or another, your Manipulator days are numbered. On this path, you'll take yourself and most of Life on Earth with you hurtling into the fiery depths or frozen wasteland of irreversible climate change.

Or you might just see that in order for you (or your children) to retain the influence or wealth you enjoy, that you (or they) need to be alive.

The Manipulator avatar derives a sense of power from exercising control over the less powerful. So the best way for *any* Player to defend against the Dark Powers is to use power healthily.

If you regularly play a Manipulator avatar, big or small, you could help turn the Game around. You could use your power, knowledge and influence to mobilise players into creating a future of health and wellbeing. Perhaps you'll recognise that healing comes from letting go of the need for control (easier said than done). Or, you'll find yourself beginning to care what happens to this beautiful, fragile world and shift your focus to ethical, profitable, business. Really… you may as well side with Life.

The Fields

You've familiarised yourself with the avatars. That's good. Getting to grips with the Game can be uncomfortable; disturbing, even. But it's vital for Life that we do.

To sum up: the Manipulator avatar is in service of the Dark Powers. The Cynic avatar scores mostly for the Dark Powers, but can sometime score for Life with a combination of good intention and high awareness. The Traditionalist avatar is loyal to traditions or the dominant establishment – and as the Dark Powers currently dominate our establishments, it usually scores for them. However, when it defends a healthy tradition it scores for Life. The Sleepwalker avatar can score for either side, but does so without intention. The Dark Powers want to keep players in this avatar, so they can be manipulated into scoring for them. Those on the side of Life are trying to wake them up. The Avoider avatar has good intention, and would score for Life if it had the Courage. The Altruist avatar is the mirror of the Cynic: it scores mostly for Life, but can sometimes score for the Dark Powers with low awareness. The Hero avatar is the mirror of the Manipulator, in service of Life.

Any reader with thoughts like 'I think I'm a Traditionalist' hasn't fully grasped yet how the avatars work. It's tempting and natural to want to affix labels, but a Player might be in Traditionalist one day, and Avoider the next. You could even be in them both at the same time: for example being vocally anti-religion, while a part of you is intrigued by spirituality but doesn't want to be seen as flaky. You're playing multiple avatars when you use social media to speak out for Life, whilst ripping apart another player for real or perceived factual inaccuracies, or an ideological difference.

You might identify particularly with one avatar, but it doesn't define you: maybe you're a habitual Cynic who sometimes plays Altruist. That doesn't mean you are 'a Cynic' or 'an Altruist'. We are all human beings, players in this Game; and we can and do move in and out of various avatars as we play. *The more aware we are, the more choice we have.*

You won't always be right about which avatar you're playing. Cynics sometimes think they're playing Manipulator, not realising they themselves are being manipulated. Or when you're less informed than you realise, you might think you're in Hero when you're actually playing Traditionalist or even Sleepwalker. And you might think you're in Altruist when you're actually playing Hero, quite unaware of what an extraordinary and courageous thing you're doing.

It's not the purpose (or the place) of this book to tell you what to do. It simply describes the Game, and invites you to assess how you're playing it. If you're open to that, these questions might be useful:

Which avatar or avatars do you play most often? Which do you never play? Are you happy with this as it is? If not, what would you like to try instead?

The next section gives information on how to play each avatar in the fields where the Game is played out. Here you will find twelve fields, laid out clearly to aid navigation, but behind the scenes they are endless; they overlap and are multi-layered. There's a short introduction to each field, a brief description of how each avatar plays it, and the current State of Play. You'll already know something about the fields; perhaps some of them more than others. You'll also see some of the fields in a way that hadn't occurred to you before, and some features will come as a complete surprise. For those who'd like to know more, there's a resource section at the end of each field suggesting films, books and websites. Some are practical, some more spiritual. And of course there are endless resources out there if you want to do your own research.

The fields are complex. Each one could easily take up a whole book. What follows is an overview of each field, giving enough information for you to choose how to play. It has been fact-checked, but if there's something you question, you'll be able to Google it and make your own mind up.

Here are some basics to keep in mind as you go through the fields.

There are two opposing forces, or energies: Life and the Dark Powers. Both of these forces are active in government, media, banking and business, but the Dark Powers tend to gather in these powerful arenas.

No field is split cleanly into sides. As we've seen, all players channel both Life and Dark Powers, and adopt multiple avatars.

Until you learn how to play the Game, you will slip in and out of avatars without conscious choice. As you develop Awareness, it gets easier to choose your own avatar. You have to be alert: your avatar will often morph without warning as you enter a new field, and it could morph within a field. And it's common to embody more than one avatar at a time. Avatar dynamics are explained more fully later on.

You can play any of the avatars in any of the fields, but there will probably be one or two that you habitually play. This could vary across the fields. You can learn to choose any avatar at any point in the Game, but hardly any players develop enough 'free will' skill to play consciously all the time. Most players, no matter how experienced, get drawn into avatars without noticing.

Some avatars might be harder to play because they are unfamiliar. The more you play them, the more natural they will become.

The fields are tricky to navigate. There are overlaps, twists and turns, hidden layers, and landmarks that keep morphing. You need to be super-mindful and highly responsive. You have to keep your eyes wide open.

Field 1: Money

> Money is a token of exchange. It helps us get the things we need to live comfortably. Not having enough makes us miserable; more than enough can make us equally unhappy. Money holds our fascination: it's become a deeply rooted symbol of power, self-worth, value, status, and influence. It also scores serious points for Life or the Dark Powers, depending what you do with it. Never underestimate the power of the purse.

THE DARK POWERS

Most regular players of the global Manipulator avatar in the Money field are in the wealthiest 1% of the population, or trying to get into it. They may be heads of corporations or big family-owned companies; top bankers, stockbrokers or media moguls; owners of world class football teams or inheritors of wealth and land originally taken from other players.

In the UK, the top 1% holds approximately 99% of the wealth in the country. They have 99 bars of chocolate while the other 99% of players divide – or fight over – the remaining one. Top CEOs' salaries are often over £5m: nearly two hundred times the average UK salary. Is that fair? That's the last question world class Manipulators will be asking. But remember, avatars are not people, or groups of people. Not all the top 1% are regular Manipulators – and not all those who play Manipulator are in that elite group.

Dark Finance, the shadow side of banking, *creates money* and then lends it to other players – with interest. Sucking up wealth and moving it around in vast, abstract sums is how they play the Game. They invest others' money in activities that involve exploitation of people and other animals, destruction of species and eco-systems; activities that contribute to climate change or pollution of air, water and land.

Those playing Manipulator within the world of Dark Finance have enormous power. But they're not usually a household name, and neither do they want to be – especially if they have lucrative but unprovable connections with drug cartels, people traffickers, arms dealers or the Mafia.

The Cynic avatar often carries out Manipulators' work: knowingly fleecing other players, for example creating or promoting financial, business or political systems that syphon Money to offshore tax havens, or running all sorts of inventive scams that target the vulnerable. They're rewarded with cash, prestige or influence for not caring how other players are affected. Experts in the field, they generally win. And as winners, they get to write the rules about how a country's finance works.

Some play Manipulator or Cynic avatars in senior finance-related positions in Dark State, the corrupt underbelly of government. Their top priority (whatever they pretend) isn't the lowest paid workers, or those on benefits, who have no money for pleasure at all. Their top priority is the 1%: that's where the power is. And they probably have their own stash of inherited wealth, shady business interests via family members, and a few offshore tax dodges going on.

In collusion with powerful Dark Finance, Dark State avoids banking reform – even though investment banks caused the crash from which so many players continue to suffer. Instead, they make the poorest pay for Dark Finance gambling games that go wrong. They perpetuate the myth of austerity, even though there's no shortage of money: the UK is one of the wealthiest countries in the world, and its government has no problem finding funds for war.

Some play the Cynic avatar getting rich through aggressive and premeditated take-overs; operating parasitic agencies of all kinds, or other 'middleman' roles; through senior posts for mates, or devising and pushing through dodgy law that benefits the powerful. They know that as a direct result of increasing inequality, they get rich while other players get redundancy, bankruptcy, homelessness, zero hours contracts, unpaid internships, pay freezes, cuts to government departments and public services.

Some even play Cynic through involvement with big charities, recognising them as potentially phenomenal money spinners. These Cynics use guilt as a tool to extract cash, often from those who can afford it least, but ate trusting and kind. Enough gets through to the actual work to keep the trustees happy, but those playing Cynic avatars manage to cream off an enormous profit along the way.

The Dark Powers score against Life in this field through greed. And we're all capable of greed. But also remember: individuals capable of playing Manipulator or hard Cynic (except true psychopaths) are all capable of playing the other avatars, and scoring for Life.

HOW TO SCORE FOR LIFE

With awareness of this Field, you know it's not only the big players who can make a difference. Playing the Altruist avatar you spend rather than hoard, keeping a healthy flow going round the Game. But you don't let your Money go to the Dark Powers. You don't sleepwalk into buying the damaging food they mass-produce, or spend all your income on the furnishings, houses, garments and devices Dark Corporation sells as if they were going out of fashion (which they are: Cynical marketing sees to that).

An Altruist avatar scores for Life by not spending with chain-stores, supermarkets or global online companies but locally, with ethical small traders whenever possible. (Anyone playing a Traditionalist avatar, rolling their eyes at the word 'ethical', here it just means 'good for Life'. Any objections?)

If you can afford to, you give to charities – checking them for corruption levels first – so they can work for Life on your behalf.

With awareness, you see through spin (and a bit of the Cynic helps here). You don't believe the myths the Dark Powers want you to believe: the lie of trickle-down economy, the fallacy of economic growth, the sham of austerity. You don't get seduced by instant loans; you recognise and reject the practice of renting Money from Dark Finance as the norm. You avoid financial transactions that would keep you in permanent debt, not fooled by adverts with nice cartoon graphics and a carefully chosen plinky little tune that Manipulators hope you will associate with childhood, trust, and freedom.

You may be a Player who's richer than most; so much richer, you truly had no idea how many players find it hard to pay their rent or feed their family, and what that daily struggle feels like. You may have no concept of what it's like to be evicted and find yourself, unbelievably, with nowhere to sleep. You've never had to queue outside a food bank, or face the stark possibility of starvation. But moving out of Sleepwalker, maybe you realised other players suffer *because* you (and others) are so wealthy, and perhaps you score for Life by finding ways to give back to society.

Playing the Avoider avatar in the Money field, you've read about families living in poverty, and you find it disturbing. You see people sleeping in doorways, and feel a pang as you cross to the other side of the street. Maybe you're lucky enough to have a higher than average income: enough to invest. You don't need to know what's happening to your money; in fact, you really don't want to know what it's being used for. It can take courage to face reality. But when you do, you can immediately begin scoring for Life in this field, if you choose, even if only a little.

Or you shift out of the Traditionalist avatar, when you no longer believe that banking is a respectable business; when you recognise that the financial crash and long recession were caused by the greed and recklessness of Dark Finance. You might move into Avoider for a while, unsure what to do now.

If you have savings and want to invest in Life, you could consider small ethical start-ups that need help to get going, maybe spreading the risk through peer-to-peer lending sites such as Funding Circle. If you want to use an established investment service, you might do your research on 'Move your Money'. You'll probably be saving with a bank such as Triodos or a local Credit Union; or with a building society, owned by its members. Playing Altruist, you find the most ethical current account out there – willing to accept that banks with principles pay less interest, because they don't profit from exploitation or destruction. You might even play Hero, challenging Dark State for bailing out investment bankers.

You can, of course, score for Life working in the financial sector, playing Altruist or Hero as you use your position to bring about a more equitable economy. You might play Altruist as shareholder of a large company: having woken up to global destruction, you're pushing directors to act more ethically. You could even be vastly wealthy, and give a lot to charity – but if your wealth is coming from damaging activities, you're playing Manipulator and Altruist simultaneously. It's complex.

Plenty of business leaders score for Life. Andrew Carnegie devoted most of his steel fortune to founding libraries and museums. More recently, Paul Lister walked away from a lucrative outdoor clothing business to develop a rewilding project on Scotland's depleted uplands. Capitalism doesn't have to be destructive: check out Copiosis for a vision that could work equitably for people and planet.

Other Heroes include Positive Money, who make players aware of how Dark Finance's corrupt monetary system actually works in the UK. In their proposed alternative economy money benefits all of society, not just the richest few. The New Economics Foundation is also developing a workable economic model that supports and enhances Life rather that destroying it.

Simon Oldridge, a former chartered accountant, used his experience to develop the Inequality Watch website. Its interactive graphics show how the UK's wealth is distributed and where you fit in – as well as dispelling the economic myths Dark State feed players through Dark Media.

Chuck Collins, author of *Born on Third Base*, was born into great wealth but gave his inheritance away. He's now dedicated to addressing inequality, pointing out that the 1% have no idea how others live, especially those who are really hard up. He calls on the wealthy to address the gap – and on everyone else to build bridges with the 1% rather than vilify and resent them. He doesn't want to see the poor wage war on the rich. He doesn't want a revolution; he wants integration.

In Totnes, the first Transition Town, the REconomy Project is a supportive, nurturing incubator for start-up enterprises and community projects, home of the Local Entrepreneur Forum and a host of other programmes aiming to support a resilient and equitable local economy.

You can score for Life in the Money field at election time, by voting for politicians who promise greater equality and a fairer pay ratio; parties that will stimulate local economies and put people and planet at the centre of their policies, rather than unsustainable economic growth. You might petition for fairer taxes and a guaranteed basic income to promote greater equality, which generally leads to greater contentment and happiness, thus scoring for Life.

Whether you have money or not you can play the Altruist avatar, find non-monetary ways of valuing and being valued: sharing, mutual exchange of food, time or help; generosity and gratitude; abundant joy in the free gifts of friendship, nature and creativity. All these zero cost activities score significantly for Life, and most help build strong community.

You could play Money Hero in your community and help build local economic resilience, and have a lot of fun doing it. You could start a local currency like the Bristol Pound, for example. REconomy will gladly give you advice. And for those who want a deep understanding of this field, Schumacher College in Devon runs a Masters in Economics for Transition.

State of Play
The Dark Powers are in a strong position. Life is making some good creative responses, but needs to gain far more ground to challenge the Dark Powers' grip. Money is consistently reliable as a Game changer, but players' awareness is generally low. We need more in Hero to start bold new initiatives. We could see a plot twist where Dark Finance wakes up and realises we can't have infinite economic growth on a depleted planet, and starts to invest in Life instead of destruction.

Resources for Life

Book: *Confessions of an Economic Hitman,* John Perkins

Book: *Sacred Economics,* Charles Eisenstein

Book: *Born on Third Base,* Chuck Collins

Book: *The Gift Economy,* Lewis Hyde

Film: *The Big Short,* Adam Mackay

Facebook: Gift Economy

Facebook: Economics of Happiness

RSA Animate: Economics is for Everyone!

Highpaycentre.org

Moveyourmoney.org.uk

Triodos.co.uk

Positivemoney.org

nef.org

Inequalitywatch.org

REconomy.org

Field 2: Education

The Education field is where players learn how to think and behave – how to play the Game. Naturally both sides want control of this field. They each want education to influence players to score for their side. What players learn will strongly influence which avatars they play and when. It's one of the most crucial fields.

THE DARK POWERS

In the Game, Education is all about producing young adults equipped to serve the great machine of the Dark Powers. It's a vital tool for maintaining the consumer culture that's destroying health, community, livelihood, ecosystems, species and habitable planet. Dark State operators are active throughout this field: lurking within the Department for Education, Ofsted and cross-party committees.

Education is used by Manipulator avatars as a vehicle for indoctrination, controlled by examinations and a rigid framework. They enforce a system that is (at its worst) tedious and depressing, stressful and all-consuming for many pupils – and many teachers.

Students play Sleepwalker in this field when they swallow everything they're taught without chewing it over, which is why it's good for the Dark Powers to get players into Sleepwalker young. The Traditionalist avatar goes along with the system, dutifully learning the facts and processes needed to pass exams (or do a particular job). Its players can then close their minds to pretty much everything else, believing they have no further need of learning.

Those playing Traditionalist are often employed within the system: devising standardised tests, defining learning outcomes, and insisting that teachers complete all the relevant paperwork. The Traditionalist is good at this work, with natural skills in sticking to protocol. (Someone was probably following protocol when they removed nature-related words including 'acorn', 'heron' and 'willow' from the Oxford Junior Dictionary, furthering a widespread severance from the natural world.)

Bit by bit, humanity is being stripped out of Education. Art History is one casualty – and this is not a 'fluffy' subject. Art is how humanity's true story, rather than the illusion the Dark Powers have created, is carried from generation to generation. Health and Social Care studies are also under threat, with obvious implications for humanity. Any Player who thinks Humanities is a 'soft' area of Education should realise that it deals with the very existence of our species. There's nothing soft about that. And for those who prefer hard data: Statistics is another subject under threat.

Steep university fees create a consumer culture of competition, entitlement and conformity rather than enabling thorough Education specifically for those who really want to study their special subject in depth. Some players, Sleepwalking into Uni because "it's what you do", use the services of a Cynical essay writer to get their degree. In a competitive world it seems like a good solution that doesn't do any harm. They might not realise it scores for the Dark Powers, undermining both truth and trust.

Some playing Manipulator have cut off funds to Adult Education: as soon as young people have been pumped full of what to know, think, and believe, they're a finished product ready to enter the economic system. Once they get a job, they'll get work-related training to fit them more exactly to their place in the system.

Dark Corporation sniffs out opportunities to make big bucks from lucrative building, technology or catering contracts in the Education field. Some run chains of academies, enjoying lavish perks at the expense of taxpaying players. Checks and balances are removed by getting rid of parent governors. Those playing hard Cynic are out to make money, or acquire power and prestige. Education just happens to be the field where there's an opportunity. They might be a head teacher who wants a High Performing school for the kudos – never mind the stress for teachers, children and parents in getting there. Never mind whether the children enjoy learning, or find their true gift, or build strong relationships. These things are only important if they affect test scores, and therefore your reputation.

A Manipulator avatar might be head of an elite public school or college, or Chancellor or Vice-Chancellor of a prestigious university. Power and kudos come naturally; their manoeuvring in elite circles means they have little interest in the daily lived experience of students.

At this point in the Game, teachers are reporting increasingly aggressive parents. But the aggression isn't usually about the forced removal and indoctrination of their children (what you'd expect in a sane world). It's mostly because the school didn't get a good Ofsted report, or the child's grades aren't what the parent hoped for. A system of fierce competition between schools and between children is bound to lead to competitive behaviours. Parents naturally want their child to go to the best school – but when they're playing Cynic it's not about the child's happiness, quality of life, or learning to live well in the world.

There has to be a better way than this. And luckily, there is.

HOW TO SCORE FOR LIFE

Most players care about the field of Education, and give it serious thought. Many question that their children spend half their waking lives absorbing facts and ideas that they as parents can't influence, let alone decide. With such awareness, you might also begin to question what they're taught (much of which they will never use) or how they're taught it (in rows, not allowed to move around or express themselves). Perhaps it starts to feel obviously wrong that Dark State can actually punish you for not making your children undergo this process every day.

As a parent playing the Altruist avatar, you don't accept the trope that your children need to be competitive to survive. You feel in your heart that learning how to collaborate and share information will be just as important for a successful and happy adulthood. You begin teaching your children very early how to score for Life in all the fields. You also teach them how to think for themselves, and help them develop a sense of self-worth, and a feeling of able to make a difference. From that secure base all other learning can happen: basic maths and language but also ecology, human relationships, health, crafts, cooking, building, engineering, gardening and so forth, and then commerce, entrepreneurship, economics, and policies that benefit Life. Some decide on home schooling for their children, to make sure they get a truly rounded education.

If you're a student, you stop the Dark Powers scoring when you refuse to accept the myth that if you aren't academic, you're a failure. You take pride in your potential as a poet, dancer, carer, cook, artisan, or visionary philosopher – or simply a kind human being who lives well in the world and with other beings.

Cynic *can* be a very positive avatar for a student to play. Playing Cynic, you don't accept being taught what to think and believe: you'd rather make up your own mind. This keeps you awake and questioning everything – something Dark State doesn't encourage. You manage to retain your own critical thought, to entertain multiple possibilities rather than one 'right answer'. However, overplaying this avatar, you run the risk of not learning anything at all (as well as making life in the classroom impossible for your teacher and classmates!)

When you bring awareness to workplace training events, you consider the corporate messages behind the teaching: how to maximise profit, apply policy, sell more stuff, or manage others. You take what's useful, leave what's not, and question anything you're unsure about. Good learning is more important to you than passing the course and ticking the box. You also check whether what you're learning is aligned with your values.

In the Altruist avatar, you continue to learn whatever you need for each new phase of your life. You might study a subject deeply; equally you might approach everything you do, and every conversation you have, as opportunities to learn.

If you work in Education, you're pushing for arts to be kept on the curriculum. You know that the future will be digital, visual and rapidly changing, so creativity and innovation will be important skills. Maybe you feel school is too controlling, teaching obedience at the expense of innovation. Maybe you believe it measures too much, and measures the wrong things. Perhaps you work at a long-established boarding school. Some of the traditions might seem ridiculous, and you suspect some of them are quite cruel. You score for Life when you speak out about a system you believe is broken; when you refuse to be silenced by the vast weight of history and tradition.

Playing Altruist, Education is about helping a learner of any age or ability toward becoming a fulfilled version of themselves. You know that with such an unpredictable future coming, today's children need to be taught fewer facts and more of how to research, experience, and make sense for themselves. You help them to develop – and you role-model – awareness, courage and collaboration. You encourage students to enquire, challenge, negotiate, meditate, dream and innovate. You teach them to use technology discerningly, and to form their own views through discussion, and from multiple sources of information and ideas.

You're there to facilitate their learning: you know what questions to ask, when to encourage, when to challenge their assumptions and encourage a range of opinions and ideas. You let them see it's healthy, not disobedient, to question what they're being taught. But you also teach discipline and respect.

You've observed that some pupils like to learn on the move, some need periods of quiet, and some like to draw or make things while they think. You acknowledge their unique ways of being, and try to support each one in what they need to thrive. Playing Altruist, you don't mind when they make mistakes. In fact you welcome it, because that's when the best learning can happen – if mistakes are seen as an opportunity to discuss and improve, rather than be shamed or stigmatised.

Perhaps inspired by schools such as West Rise Junior in Eastbourne, you encourage outdoor learning about guided risk, and our place in the natural world. You slip in as much joy and adventure as possible, even if it means taking paperwork home. You teach the curriculum as necessary, while others score for Life by working to undo standardised curriculum and standardised testing, knowing there is no such thing as a standard child. You might work outside the system, where you can encourage children of different ages to learn from and with each other, and don't have to divide learning into classes separate 'subjects', when in reality most activities draw on a broad range of knowledge and skills

You're playing the Hero avatar if you're working to wake other players up to the damage done in the Education system, actively promoting healthier ways of learning. Noam Chomsky, one of today's great thinkers, can be seen playing Hero, explaining how the system is so destructive to Life. Ken Robinson is another Hero articulating his Ted Talk vision of Education based on creativity (which he defines as 'having ideas with some value'). Writer and psychologist Malcolm Parlett suggests that children and adults need to learn 'whole intelligence' rather than only academic subjects. He shows in his book *Future Sense* how this can work for anyone of any age – and indeed is vital to meet the challenges of tomorrow.

A small group of frustrated parents played a collective Hero avatar when they began the movement Let our Kids be Kids, in response to increasingly punishing testing. It grew phenomenally, and now (amongst other significant accomplishments) provides parental peer support for those trying to find the courage to challenge the system.

There are establishments across the UK doing Heroic work; educating for Life. The Centre for Alternative Technology in Wales is an innovative showcase of practical, sustainable design. It offers residential courses as well as hands-on learning for visitors. Hampshire's Sustainability Centre is on a similar educational mission, teaching crafts and skills that benefit Life. Wildwise is one of several organisations teaching children and adults vital skills for living in the natural world, and at Schumacher College in Devon, you could spend the morning learning about quantum physics, the afternoon harvesting salad leaves and the evening participating in a knicker-making workshop.

Hawkwood College for adults has creativity at the heart of its programme, and is home of the Centre for Future Thinking, a platform for exploring and sharing creative responses to tomorrow's challenges. The Small School, founded by Satish Kumar, bases secondary Education around community and trust, teaching small classes student-based skills for heart, mind and hands. Steiner Schools and Forest Schools consciously educate for wellbeing, both of the child and for Life.

At Embercombe near Exeter, Mac Macartney and colleagues run courses for adults, helping each unique person discover how best they can act for Life. Drawing on his profound learning experiences with indigenous people, Mac founded Embercombe on his conviction that society has lost connection with the essential Life principles of connectedness, belonging, and responsibility. Mac humbly yet powerfully embodies the role of wise elder in Education: a living reminder that this role has been almost universally replaced with a false position of authority based on knowledge and control rather than wisdom.

If you're working a sixty hour week, building creativity and outdoor time into a strict curriculum and *still* managing to complete all the paperwork, you're playing the Hero avatar. If you're keeping arts and humanities alive in Education, you're playing Hero. If you're a parent who resists the pressure and keeps your small child from SATS tests, you're playing Hero. And if you're a student holding on to your individuality, despite pressure from the system – you're playing Hero.

State of Play
Despite the light held by many individual players in this field, The Dark Powers have hijacked education. Life suffers as a result – from a personal to a planetary level. Luckily most educators are natural Altruists. More and more want to reclaim Education, but Heroes must find more creative and effective ways to break the increasing stranglehold of the Dark Powers.

Resources for Life

Book: *Expansive Education*, Guy Claxton
Book: *Future Sense*, Malcolm Parlett
Facebook/twitter: Michael Rosen
Facebook: Let our Kids be Kids
TED talks: Ken Robinson (various)
YouTube: Noam Chomsky (various)
Home-education.org.uk
Cat.org.uk (Centre for Alternative Technology)
Sustainability-centre.org
Schumachercollege.org.uk
Hawkwoodcollege.co.uk
Embercombe.org
Steinerwaldorf.org
Forestschools.com
Wildwise.co.uk

Field 3: Media

You are what you eat; you are also what you read and watch. What you take into your body *becomes* your body, and what you absorb from the Media *becomes* your mind and even your soul, forming your understanding and your values. Societal norms in the Game are shaped almost entirely by Media: no wonder so many Media outlets are heavily controlled by Dark Powers.

THE DARK POWERS

Dark Media (the shady aspect of communication) is the Manipulator's playground: opportunities for exploitation are ripe, lucrative and easy picking. The Dark Powers use all forms of media to push their agenda to a Sleepwalking public. Adam Curtis' gripping documentary *HyperNormalisation* offers one informed story about what lies behind the illusion spun by the Dark Powers.

We do know that a few multi-billionaires own over 70% of the UK's papers, and most satellite TV. Their businesses are registered offshore, so they don't pay tax in the UK (although they goad players into resenting 'benefit scroungers'). Manipulator avatars choose editors prepared to play Cynic and promote fear, hatred, and spitefulness. Through the printed word, TV screen and online, they have no problem coaxing players into Sleepwalker with a dangerous, carefully designed world of shallow selfishness and conformity – dressing it all up as entertainment.

Dark Media feeds opinions to Traditionalist avatars. When Heroes publicly challenge Manipulators, Dark Media label them as 'conspiracy theorists'… and the Traditionalist does love a label. Dark Corporation has power over Dark Media: editors playing Cynic don't want to upset wealthy advertisers, so they're careful how they present environmental news implicating corporations (or they look the other way completely). Mainstream news focuses almost exclusively on death, destruction and corruption, ignoring all the good that happens every day in the world. And yet although many players are depressed by mainstream news, many feel an odd compulsion to watch it. No wonder so many are stuck in Avoider, feeling there's no point in trying to make a difference. And so the Dark Powers continue to up their score of destruction.

Dark Media Manipulators have a close relationship with Downing Street, using privileged access to MPs to dictate policy. Rupert Murdoch, when asked why he was so anti-EU, said, "That's easy. When I go into Downing Street they do what I say; when I go to Brussels they take no notice."

Dark Media is growing daily more powerful than the UK government, forcing its hand on matters of great national significance such as Brexit. Nobody knows exactly how they got to hold such power, but it's clear they're untouchable, publishing headlines daily that incite racial hatred and violence, despite legislation that prohibits this.

A lot of players trust the BBC: it's been around all their lives, and probably longer. They don't realise how far the influence of Dark State and Dark Corporation has permeated the BBC's news department. But the Dark Powers are scoring large in the BBC, through TV or radio news editors who yield to pressure to bias coverage. Heroes defending Life in the public arena are typically portrayed as weird, bad, or losers – or non-existent. And Sleepwalkers lap it up.

Cynical editors set up political interviews and camera angles like puppeteers. Their job is to undermine Heroes who either don't know it's happening, or feel they have to go along with it rather than lose their mainstream media platform. They're out-manoeuvred either way.

Cynics in this field present 'balanced debates' in which they give airspace to those who (for financial gain) pretend climate change isn't happening. Sleepwalker and Traditionalist avatars believe the lie. Aggressive and insulting political figures get huge attention, whilst major speeches and enormous rallies of politicians defending Life go unreported.

Players in Avoider know perfectly well that amidst all the trivial entertainment, Dark Media is lying. They might feel uncomfortable, but carry on watching and reading anyway. In public they go along with the rhetoric, to stay part of the In group. And believe me, the Dark Powers know how very important this is to players. *They created the In group, and they milk it for all it's worth.* With chilling ease, they manipulate players into despising Heroes who are trying to defend people and planet, by making Hero-hatred not only acceptable, but fashionable.

Manipulators pay Cynics to hack mobile phones, spread misinformation on social media, promote Dark Corporation's goods in columns disguised as journalism. They whip up public confusion by turning the accusation of 'fake news' back on independent new sites, so that no-one knows what to believe.

Some journos go into areas of great suffering like obliterated villages or mud-swamped refugee camps, and then play detached Cynic, depicting victims as 'parasites'. This attitude is absorbed by players in Sleepwalker; it emboldens those in Traditionalist and Cynic to be openly hostile and vicious, and drags those playing Avoider into a norm they're reluctant to be part of, but are anyway.

TV entertainment gets absorbed too: 'gritty' dramas have viewers riveted by the cynicism, the disconnected or damaging sex, the image-crafting; soaps, that are supposed to reflect our culture actually create it; reality shows debase Life; fictions turn us into children delighted by fairy tales rather than alert, questioning adult members of community.

Inevitably (deliberately?), TV shapes players' values, and therefore how we play the Game: ideas about what is okay, or even desirable, in society. Lying and cheating, self-harm, hard porn, rape, violence, drug-taking, and even serial killing are normalised. Sleepwalking viewers assume and imagine that under a polite surface, everyone is violent; everyone wants sex devoid of affection or even respect, as portrayed on their screens every evening. Relationships are sexualised before they're emotionally ready, and friendly advances are misinterpreted as a sexual come-on. Society's collective sense of Right and Wrong is eroded; mistrust and wariness ensue, and so the Dark Powers score more.

Some play 'home Manipulator' orchestrating hate campaigns on social media: online communities for Cynic and Traditionalist avatars to sign up to the Dark Powers. You know you're playing Avoider when you have a friend or family member who challenges the Dark Powers or supports Heroes on social media, and you warn them to "be careful"; or when you agree with their posts but dare not 'like' them for fear of what others will think. Habitual players of Hero or Altruist avatars often get drawn into Cynic, taking part in angry and vitriolic exchanges… and the Dark Powers score.

They also score through news sites with profit, not truth, as their main goal. For the Cynic avatar, there's a good income from ads if you can generate enough traffic. Facts are no longer required, or even appreciated. As long as a story sells copy, or attracts clicks, who cares whether it's true?

The Dark Powers use their Media position to *create* the Game, seeding memes that would seem to guarantee their triumph. If we believe their trope, the Dark Powers have taken us into a post-truth age – but this is only true if we allow it.

Recently, smear campaigns haven't been working as the Dark Powers anticipated. In fact, the more vicious their attacks on Life, the more players seem to flip into Altruist or Hero, using social media to spread creative responses on Life's behalf.

In 2016 a few Heroes began a movement called 'Stop Funding Hate'. This now powerful and successful social media campaign calls out companies whose adverts appear on tabloid front pages alongside hate propaganda. It's a great example of what people can do when governments fail to act. When companies such as Paperchase and Pizza Hut began to withdraw their ads from the tabloids, Dark Media lashed back (with the help of Boris Johnson from representing Dark State) in a concerted attack on Stop Funding Hate, attempting to discredit their work and minimise their popularity. But many thousands of players took Hero and Altruist avatars, in a push-back for Life.

If you'd been Sleepwalking in this Field, you might only now be noticing the disconnect when a news item on climate change is followed by a piece on growth in GDP as a positive thing. You might begin to think it strange that the daily news gives you the latest stock market and currency figures, but not the latest rise in global temperature or carbon in the atmosphere. If you're playing Avoider, you manage to shrug and carry on as if everything was fine (even though you know it really isn't). But you can no longer ignore runaway climate change, if you want to be on the side of Life.

You know that whatever Facebook or Google show you is based on your previous activity, and that your worldview is shaped from those articles and posts. So maybe you regularly check out news sites that challenge your thinking. You know most players in Traditionalist, Sleepwalker or Avoider avatars don't see posts that might wake them up or encourage them to score for Life, so you find ways to engage in Facebook discussion with those who hold different views – perhaps on popular politically neutral pages. Of course, such discussions need patience and tact – or they can escalate into exchanges that don't serve you or Life.

With your new post-sleepwalking awareness, you realise how depressed, repelled, afraid or bored you actually were by constant media input. You choose your content rather than passively absorb it – or you go and do something more fulfilling or enjoyable instead. Away from the constant images of violence, you regain a healthier sense of normality than the vile fake world that Dark Media habituated you to.

Perhaps you've noticed your attention span has shrunk, and you know it's because of the dumbed down TV and magazines, and bite-sized social media. To save your brain, you begin to step back from a world of soundbites, memes and flashing images where a thousand-word blog seems long.

You might choose to play Altruist on social media, recognising it as a global tool for countering the Dark Powers. You 'like' or share whatever you believe scores points for Life – trying to keep that delicate balance just the right side of players getting bored or overwhelmed by your posts and hiding them. There are probably friends on your contact list who are Sleepwalking through certain fields (as we all are), and your posts offer a different perspective to those who are being manipulated daily by Dark Media. Plus, you get to see how others outside your circle are experiencing and describing the world. However playing Altruist, there's a risk of unwittingly share inaccurate memes of misinformation, because you agree in your heart with the core message. This contributes to a bewildering world of contradictory information in which nothing can be trusted. You need to fact-check, and keep your awareness high, to score for Life in this field.

Freed from the paralysis of Avoider, you realise you don't have to go along with trolling Heroes – or any other player. If you hear them being badmouthed, or see them attacked on Facebook, you no longer join in.

perhaps you're liberated by discovering that you can just be kind, ignoring the propaganda. You might even play Hero, and take it on.

Wit eyes open, you now know mainstream media just gives an 'establishment' take on a very select number of myriad events happening in the world. You don't accept that 'news' is something that only comes from traditional sources. Playing Cynic in this field can be helpful: in this avatar, you know perfectly well Dark Media is lying. Your news comes from your networks and your immediate surroundings, as well as independent sites such as The Canary, who publish events from around the world that mainstream Dark Media pretend aren't happening. But you're discerning, and check sources.

You can also score for Life by following sites such as Positive News and the Good News Network, beacons of light in a field so dominated by the Dark Powers. With knowledge that other players everywhere are scoring for Life every day, your view of the Game becomes more balanced. You notice that you feel happier. Hope suddenly seems much more realistic, and action more possible. And for a satirical take that gives you a laugh as well as calling out the Dark Powers, there are sites such as Southend News Network, and Newsthump.

If you choose to step into the Hero avatar in the Media field, you'll need Courage: the battle for players' minds is a fierce one. You'll need to be canny enough to uncover lies, adept and accurate with facts, skilful at writing them up in a way that speaks to people authentically and powerfully amongst all the bullshit of spin, and courageous enough to risk annoying some of the most powerful people in the world. Anna Politkovskaya was assassinated in 2006 for her human rights investigatory journalism.

Playing the Hero avatar in Media, you'll be publicly calling out the Manipulators who are wreaking environmental catastrophe, profiting from war, abusing humans and other animals, or exploiting the political system for power and status. When Dark Media publish damaging lies, you instantly call them out. No wonder they want you to stop.

In the US, Deia Schlosberg and Amy Goodman are journalists and film-makers who played Hero documenting the use of military force at peaceful protests over the Dakota pipeline (a struggle between Life and the Dark Powers watched by the world). They were arrested for their reporting – a move that took the 'civilised' world another step further away from democracy.

Journalist Nafeez Ahmed took the Heroic step of creating crowdfunded Insurge Intelligence, 'people powered watchdog journalism for the global commons', exposing Dark Powers for the sake of the common good. George Monbiot, Aditya Chakrabortty, Naomi Klein, Owen Jones and many others step regularly into the Media Hero role with articles and books directly challenging Dark State.

The list of Media Heroes is long, honourable and growing. Franny Armstrong, Adam Curtis and Michael Moore make films that expose Dark Corporation. Jonathan Pie makes spoof TV news reports that rip the hell out of Dark Media. Russell Brand makes The Trews, maverick exposés of Dark Media propaganda, ripping away the illusion woven so carefully by the Dark Powers. Mark Steel and Frankie Boyle use their comedy platform to poke fun at Dark State.

Films for Action collect subversive films and articles and share them with the world, and plenty of Heroes manage to score for Life through mainstream radio and TV. Broadcaster and veteran Player of the Hero avatar Michael Rosen uses his social media profile to challenge the Dark Powers, especially in the field of Education. His impartiality as a broadcaster is impeccable, but that doesn't necessarily protect you: BBC reporter Danny Carpenter was suspended for venting his fury with Dark State on Facebook.

You could play 'home Hero' in this field, monitoring Dark Media's output carefully so you can spot discrepancies; challenging lies, and staying informed about the Dark Powers' strategies.

Anyone could start a hashtag that becomes a movement for Life, just as

Patrisse Cullors did with *#blacklivesmatter* and Alyssa Milano with *#metoo*. You have no idea how big it might get, but you know not everyone's going to applaud.

If you feel scared to publicly challenge the Dark Powers in a public forum but you do it anyway, you're playing Hero and scoring for Life. When you express support for someone the press are ripping apart for doing good – you're playing Hero, and scoring for Life.

> ### State of Play
> Dark Media have dominated this field for many years, using it to manipulate and dumb down players for commercial and political ends. But the internet has made it possible for Altruists and Heroes to fight back; scores for Life have been surging up. Until the Dark Powers close down or fully control the internet, Life could even move into the lead through connected players. And that would be a game changer.

Resources for Life

Book: *Power without Responsibility*, Curran and Seaton
YouTube: Rich Media, Poor Democracy; Jonathan Pie; The Trews
Film: *HyperNormalisation*, Adam Curtis
Facebook: Stop Funding Hate
Facebook/Twitter: Michael Rosen
Monbiot.com
Filmsforaction.com
Positive.news
Goodnewsnetwork.org
Newsthump.com
Thecanary.co
Michaelmoore.com
Snopes.com
Biffvernon.blogspot.co.uk

Field 4: Technology

Technology is a tricky field of rapid and far-reaching changes. Brilliant minds have innovated advances that have built on themselves, bringing cloning, virtual and augmented reality, robots and artificial intelligence. Understanding of implications can't keep up with innovations. Technology offers great possibilities for both Life and the Dark Powers. With new developments emerging so fast, we need to make sure we get it right for each tomorrow.

THE DARK POWERS

The Dark Powers make use of Technology to dominate the Game. Hierarchy and conflict have existed throughout history, but technological advances have made war, surveillance, mind control and environmental destruction possible on a grand scale. *That's why this is a crucial field, at a crucial stage of the Game.*

The Dark Powers deploy communication technology to keep players where they want them: in Sleepwalker or Avoider for working or shopping, or triggering Cynic or Traditionalist to turn them against each other. Meanwhile there are also rogue Manipulators busy developing viruses and malware for personal satisfaction.

Manipulators instruct some players to monitor and collect data on other players, making them easier to manipulate (and control, if needed). Dark State justifies surveillance technology, as it's also used to great effect to prevent terrorist attacks.

The Dark Powers are pushing for laws that would give them economical and technical advantages over other internet users. Online connection is where the future of the Game will be shaped, and those who control the means of connection wield the power. Some believe a global data failure in 2016 originated in Russia or China as a practise run for taking out the internet; cyberwar could also mean attacks on power stations, and the great machine of the UK's financial world.

The Cynic avatar is quick to see and exploit opportunities constantly opening up in the technology field, for example the get-rich-quick business of devices, bringing out new 'must-have' models with increasing frequency. Never mind the toxic lakes and slave labour, the vast acres of despoiled landfill as sleepwalking players throw 'obsolete' models away.

Some profit from internet porn, creaming income from isolation and screen dependence that can lead to physical or psychological sexual harm, emotional disconnect and shame. Meanwhile, others profit from the industry of social media content moderation. The worst videos and images of violation are browsed and deleted by poorly paid staff in the Philippines; teams of counsellors help them deal with the trauma. The Cynic avatar is okay with profiting from this industry: someone has to do it. Some might say they're playing Hero.

Technology itself has detached many players from real life: enabling anonymity, cutting off empathy and personal responsibility, encouraging us to be hard, selfish and even aggressive. In a 'swipe left' culture we can dismiss others without the discomfort that moderates and softens face-to-face rejection. Most vehicles are designed so that we feel untouchable, creating the sense that we can get our own way. Technology such as virtual reality takes that detachment a step further, giving players a false sense of power over others. For many who feel disempowered in the Game, this is a seductive option. But when humanity is treated as disposable, the Dark Powers score and Life loses.

If you can't resist addiction to your screen even though you know it's damaging your health and relationships, you're in the Avoider avatar. If

Technology blinds you to real Life around you, or if you passively receive information more than you think for yourself, you're Sleepwalking.

Elsewhere in this broad field, Manipulators use the threat of advanced weapons technology to keep other countries submissive. They maintain cripplingly expensive nuclear deterrent systems to demonstrate their power. Dark State claims this is to protect Life, but meanwhile Life suffers every day as money is siphoned off by the huge military branch of Dark Corporation.

Like most technological developments, biomimicry is a double-edged sword. It models objects on biological organisms or processes, which is a smart approach as such refinements evolved and were perfected over billions of years. But borrowing from nature is corrupted when it's used to wipe out whole villages.

Arms professionals manufacture drones and other sophisticated means of killing other players without going anywhere near them, and not for self-defence. They liaise with Dark State in order to sell deathly Technology to violent regimes. Meanwhile, maverick individuals hack DNA to create super-bugs, creating the possibility of a very different third world war.

Some play Cynic developing technology such as 3-D printing or automation, knowing it will make money for the Dark Powers but put a lot of players out of work. (If you hope it will free players up to live creative and healthy lives on a guaranteed basic income, then you're in Altruist and scoring for Life.)

This is a tricky field. In it, players (maybe except the true psychopaths) are capable of scoring for both Life and Destruction, and intention isn't always enough to ensure you score for the side you mean to score for.

If you've been Sleepwalking through this field, you may not have thought about how brilliantly technology works for Life. Connection enables collaboration that makes it possible to counter the Dark Powers, availability of once-hidden information, surfacing hidden issues such as mental illness and domestic abuse, sharing all the good and joyful things happening in the world; countless ways of benefiting humanity and the whole world.

But what you might also wake up to is eye-tracking technology that records which ads you look at, and new ways to suggest products to you visually through Google Glass, or by narrow beams of verbal suggestions, or by connected children's *toys*. You realise the US National Security Agency can see every Gmail, Messenger conversation, and spreadsheet in Google docs – and actively searches them, ostensibly for terrorist threats. You become aware of the fierce, technically complex battle between Hero and Manipulator avatars over private data.

Anonymous are a group of hacktivists who take down websites belonging to organisations they believe to be perpetrating destruction: such diverse targets as Isis, Japanese whalers and child pornography sites. The group is globally dispersed, and members unidentifiable. This anonymity makes it possible to hack sites and expose corruption – but also to carry out acts of cyber-terrorism. In such a loosely dispersed and secretive group, it's hard to tell who is playing Hero.

Whistle-blower Edward Snowden exposed Dark State surveillance activity he witnessed while working for the CIA, and he's been taking refuge from retribution in Russia ever since. Maverick Julian Assange's company WikiLeaks uses technology to expose corrupt actions of Dark State, Dark Finance and Dark Corporation through leaked documents. The Dark Powers moved swiftly to discredit him, linking him with Russia, so that players don't know who to believe any more. There is of course potential for Assange, Snowden and others to score for the Dark

Powers with their disclosures; it's a considered risk they have chosen to take.

Perhaps you manage to escape constant exposure to information technology. Maybe permanent social media, a 24 hour news cycle, constant emails, and endless websites to explore, were literally too much for your brain to handle. It started shutting areas down so it could cope, like a tree sacrificing branches in times of stress. Maybe you felt frozen; unable to make decisions, unable to remember random facts such as your PIN, or tasks such as switching off the oven.

Your soul cried out for freedom from information. The only way you could get back to a 'normal' you'd almost forgotten was to stop the overload. So you cut down or cut out social media, took an offline holiday, got rid of the TV, had silence in the car, or quit your job – whatever measures were needed for you to get back to healthy mental functioning. Maybe you've decided you won't buy any new devices until yours are broken beyond repair. With a small but sustained tweak to your habits (and perhaps some discipline), you freed yourself from the paralysis of the Avoider.

The Traditionalist avatar doesn't find change easy. So playing it in Technology, one of the fastest evolving fields, is uncomfortable: you could find yourself stuck in denial. This avatar helps keep the brakes on in a field where things are moving faster than our ability to predict consequences. Playing Traditionalist, you might perform a valuable role in stopping the Dark Powers scoring. But you also risk putting the brakes on vital development that could save the Game.

You could play Altruist in this field by working on new technology such as smart refrigerators with apps that keep stock levels exactly right; using your skills to reduce food waste. And if you profit from your invention, that doesn't make you a Cynic: profit, remember, can score for Life. Or, perhaps you volunteer skills and free time to open source projects, such as software creation, or the design of something like Riversimple's eco-car.

You might be developing or supporting technologies to benefit Life, such as solar catalysts that can turn water into hydrogen, or water catalysts that can turn carbon dioxide into ethanol. But you're doing it with as much awareness as possible. Throughout the history of the Game, players have dedicated careers (and sometimes whole lives) to technology from pesticides to petrol engines, electricity to radiation, believing they could only benefit Life. Such tools, as we have learned, can obviously score for both sides, depending on the intention of their users.

When Tim Berners-Lee invented the worldwide web, he meant it to be a platform for sharing and collaboration. Yet ironically it's become dominated by a very few companies: Google, Amazon, Twitter and Facebook (and Baidu and Alibaba in China). The internet is a tool for Dark Corporation – but also makes it possible for small-scale, low-impact farmers to sell direct to their customers.

A group called the Yes Men, who believe that lies can expose truth, spent months setting up fake Dark Corporation websites. They got themselves invited to public events, where they could apologise 'on the company's behalf' for damage such as the Dow Chemical disaster in Bhopal which killed thousands, and injured many more. Controversially, the media reported that Dow would pay compensation to survivors. Meanwhile in the USA, those at snopes.com carefully research and debunk online urban myths – including what sometimes prove to be false accusations against Dark Powers. Of course when this happens, the Dark Powers score.

If you work with technology, to score for Life you'll be learning from history: trying to build in safeguards that ensure your technology won't get into the hands of Dark Powers, and ways to mitigate if it does. You might be working on nuclear fusion as a clean source of energy, mindful that nuclear fission started out the same way. However there are no guarantees: that's why your work takes courage. Maybe you're working on technology for modifying weather, or for sucking carbon out of the atmosphere. It's impossible to tell how they will play out. If they save Life when nothing else could, you'll be a retrospective Hero. If they distract us from making necessary changes to consumption in society, you'll turn out to have been Sleepwalking. You might play Hero by looking like a crackpot as you warn your company's directors about a potential danger you've identified.

You could be developing tiny robots to pollinate plants, racing to create a solution to the danger of bee population collapse. Technology is a complex area where avatars and fields overlap. To score for Life effectively, you need awareness of complexity. You need to understand consequences not as linear cause and effect but as cycles, and as complex networks with feedback loops. You act with a blend of good judgment and intuition, and always with the intention of scoring for Life. No-one knows for sure how this Technology will be used in the future. You hope it might save the Game, or at least keep Life in the Game for a little longer.

Playing Altruist in this field, you consciously use technology (or not) to score for Life. For example, you might not own many garden power tools, preferring to work your muscles, heart and lungs, and exercise skill and discretion in working slowly and carefully with nature, rather than pulling out a piece of kit that's expensive, noisy, energy-consuming and often brutal. However if you're unable to operate heavy manual tools but still want to garden, perhaps you judge that overall, that piece of kit helps you score for Life. There's no right or wrong here: there's just your choice.

The Institute for Ethics and Emerging Technology play Hero and Altruist avatars in this field. They believe that technological progress can be good for human development, as long as technologies are safe and equitably distributed. They do good work – but focus mostly on human wellbeing, neglecting the impact of technology on other species. This is a mistake for two reasons.

First, all living beings are part of an interconnected network; to consider ethics only for humans is to clear the way for lateral damage, so that ultimately we destroy the web of Life of which we are a part. Second, science is now catching up with what humans always knew until a few thousand years ago: other species have awareness, and can communicate, and form relationships. When considering the impact of technology it's clearly more ethical (as well as prudent) to include all living beings.

Humans have an amazing capacity for developing new Technology, and yet we've brought ourselves to the very brink of survival. Our design skills are only any good if we can design a society that can live in peace, wellbeing and abundance on a planet of finite resources.

State of Play
As fast as Manipulators develop new technology to take control of the Game, Heroes counter it. Manipulators respond... giving us the fastest moving field. It's a tricky field, full of paradoxes. Technology could save the Game, or could end it. In this field, Life urgently needs technically skilled players. The next generation of Hero and Altruist avatars is coming through... thankfully, as this field needs wisdom and vision.

Resources for Life

Book: *Techno-fix*, Michael Huesseman
Book: *Love and Sex with Robots*, David Levy
Book: *The Seventh Sense*, Joshua Cooper Ramo
Magazine: The New Scientist
Film: The Yes Men Fix the World, Bichlbaum, Bonanno & Engfehr
Film: *Her*, Spike Jonze
YouTube: The Simulation Hypothesis
Facebook: Anonymous
Ieet.org (Institute for Ethics and Emerging Technologies)
Phys.org
Ivpn.net (protecting online security)
Fairphone.com
Riversimple.com

Field 5: Work

Work began as action that supports and enhances Life. But the Dark Powers have changed the meaning of work: they've sucked out its soul. Most adults in the UK don't enjoy their jobs; our planet is overheating, choking and drowning through human endeavour. Players are manipulated into a system that directs their energy, creativity and intelligence into the service of the Dark Powers. But work can be fulfilling and joyful, and Life-enhancing.

THE DARK POWERS

Work is a field ripe for exploitation. The Dark Powers orchestrate a modern form of slavery, having created a work field that exploits so many players. Stress and poverty might not be *intended*, but the system pushes countless workers as far as they can go – and often beyond.

Dark Corporation (the destructive aspect of business) ravages the land, monopolises the marketplace and depletes local economies, leaving vital town centres, where humanity thrives, semi-abandoned. The work of countless human beings, directed by the Dark Powers, causes epic scale deforestation, carbon emission, plastic pollution of land and oceans, poisoning of soil and water, suffering and exploitation of humans and other animals.

Most players feel they have no option but to get a job within the system, often meaning the degradation of mind-numbing, soul-destroying work that squashes their natural joy and creativity, and achieves little of benefit to Life. Players in Traditionalist and Sleepwalker generally accept the message that jobs and employment are a good thing – missing the important piece: that work is only good if it's good for the people doing it, and achieves something positive in the world. These avatars also accept goals, procedures and standards without question – even when they are measuring and assessing the wrong things, as they so often are. The Dark Powers make bad work seem necessary and useful.

Manipulators within Dark State liaise with powerful corporate lobbyists. They might take the shape of an ex-government minister, making use of their knowledge and influence from motives of greed. Or they might be official ministerial 'buddy' to a big multinational, co-opted to protect and further their interests, introducing tax and planning laws that support Dark Corporation and squeeze small traders. They base the nation's work on a Dark Finance model of perpetual economic growth (obviously impossible on a planet of limited resources) when they could be enabling work that scores for Life. Smaller Manipulator avatars operate in the workplace at all levels, by playing ruthless power games, exploiting people and systems to get and keep control.

You're playing Cynic when you seek the best paid work you can get, regardless of the harm it does: negotiating crushing contracts with farmers, making toxic chemicals, exploiting migrants, creating ads for junk foods, throwing families out of their homes, operating intensive pig units, trading in illegal drugs, managing sex workers. (The last two are illegal and the others aren't, but they all do vast harm.)

A lot of Cynic avatars make a living from outsourcing: ruthless car park operator, manager of a detention centre, 'work capability' manager. You're playing Cynic if you drive a culture of efficiency and ruthlessness towards other players, and that's the culture you expect staff to abide by; you're playing Traditionalist when you enforce this culture because it's 'the rules'. Both Cynic and Traditionalist avatars derive pleasure from the power of enforcement bestowed on them by those higher up.

Cynics also engage in parasitic activities that suck cash from a fearful, mistrustful society, from others' industry, skills or misfortune: selling unnecessary insurance, creaming off others' profits for doing very little as an 'agent', running payday loan schemes or cold call scams, hacking bank accounts, milking charities.

Some play Cynic by playing the system: claiming benefits and working for pay on the side, making it harder for those who are genuinely struggling. Others operate in trade unions, inciting members to greed and aggression beyond what's necessary. We know it's possible to play more than one avatar at a time. Individual players scoring for the Dark Powers through work are often simultaneously scoring for Life in other fields – or even within the same field.

HOW TO SCORE FOR LIFE

Maybe you pay other people to raise your children, cook your meals, make your furniture and entertain you. Most of us do. If you love your job, and trust the players providing these services, it might be the perfect lifestyle for you. Otherwise, you might feel your life has been outsourced: that the Dark Powers have wiped out mutually supportive communities. You're in Avoider if you're not happy about this, but not prepared to step off the career ladder. Your soul urges that this is *wrong*, but something holds you there. It's worth asking: could you free yourself if you were prepared to make some courageous choices?

The best way to score for Life in this field is to find work aligned with your values, that draws on your best skills, and achieves something positive in the world. Because the Dark Powers are present, or at least latent, in all of us, no work is ever 100% positive. But when you aim to score for Life through your work as often as possible, you contribute significantly to countering the Dark Powers.

Maybe one day you reach a crossroads of purpose, of your identity. Perhaps you realise you're sick of the stress, the lack of fulfilment or the exhaustion of your current job. You don't want to feel like this any more – and you don't want to take how you feel back into your family or community. With awareness, you recognise this time of upheaval as something you need to pass through, perhaps with some collaboration, to reach a positive new beginning.

You might find the motivation (or courage) to leave a job you don't enjoy, freeing yourself from the paralysis of the Avoider avatar. Perhaps you wake up to the realisation that you work in a destructive industry: for example, mass global transport of goods. Suddenly, you can no longer accept that constant noise and pollution from planes, trucks and container ships is 'just the way the world works'. There has to be a better, less destructive way.

Maybe your work involved plastic packaging, burning oil, waste of paper resources or routine use of toxic chemical products; or it directed wealth towards the already wealthy, so depriving others. Maybe you were working with people you wouldn't choose to spend time with, in an environment you found unpleasant, doing tedious, unhealthy or stressful tasks. You realised you were only staying because any job felt better than no job; like staying in an unhappy relationship because it's better than no relationship.

Perhaps you play Traditionalist in a role such as Governance, Human Resources or Health and Safety: you're there to uphold the system, enforce the rules. Your work saves money, saves the company from legal action, or even saves lives. But depending who you work for, you maybe realise one day that your work also creates measures and targets that cost so much in stress, time and energy that they score more points for the Dark Powers than for Life. The Traditionalist avatar is a natural guardian, upholder and implementer. There are plenty of ways it can score for Life when its players are committed to structures that do good rather than harm.

Or you may be a skilful craftsperson, artisan, designer or engineer making cheap, uniform goods designed for a short life. You find such denigration of your skills heart-breaking. How can you take pride in something you're knowingly making to be thrown away? You look at going self-employed, but Dark Corporation has swallowed up your market: why would you try to make and sell beautiful unique plates, when everyone buys the 'in' shape and colour for £1.99 from the supermarket? But then you find a community in which enough players are committed to supporting each other's trades – and discover there's someone willing to share a kiln. And you're away, suddenly brimming with creative ideas.

Because the Dark Powers dominate the work field, there are more players looking for good work than there are good jobs (jobs good for you and Life). So starting your own business, or workers' co-operative, or social enterprise, or peer-funded project could be the best way if you want to score for Life with your work. Dark State, Dark Finance and Dark Corporation make starting your own venture harder than it should be. It takes courage, and so is the act of a Hero avatar. But it's a lot easier with collaboration.

You won't have to look far to find people happy to help. You'll find them online, or amongst other local traders – particularly in a Transition Town. The Transition movement is all about developing resilient, self-sufficient communities: collaboration is at the heart of the model. There's probably a Transition community near you.

In Devon, Transition project REconomy runs an annual Local Entrepreneurs Forum to help small businesses get started. A community of 'friendly dragons' assess projects and invite contributions of cash, mentoring, practical help, land, office space or whatever players have to offer. There's a positive vibe of connection and engagement, and the concept is spreading. You could hold a Local Entrepreneurs' Forum for your district: REconomy will gladly give you advice.

However, once you've started a venture to score for Life, it's quite possible that you'll slip into Sleepwalker. In your natural desire for growth, maybe you forget to keep an eye on the balancing act between profit and ethics. All enterprises have their natural full-grown size, and their natural lifespan. With sufficient awareness you notice when your business reaches either: ethical compromises creep in, relationships become stretched, and the joy and ease are gone. This stage of your venture has reached completion; you find both the courage and discipline to let it go, ready for the next idea to emerge.

Self-employment isn't for everyone on the side of Life. Some prefer to do what they can within the organisation they work for. Others knowingly take the long view, working for a company that causes damage through its activities in order to gain the funds, contacts or experience needed to begin their own business that will benefit Life. They're playing Cynic and Hero avatars simultaneously.

If you can't or don't want to leave the job you're in, you can find opportunities to help Life anyway. Whether you're in retail, manufacturing, the police force, a detention centre, a supermarket, a job centre or a call centre, you make a point of kindness to colleagues and anyone else your work brings you into contact with – even if you risk getting into trouble for being kind.

If you're willing to risk stepping into Hero, you challenge damaging practices in your workplace and create positive alternatives, changing the system from within. You might be on your company's sustainability project team. You're a role model at work: a Life force. If you're tasked with making the charity or government department you work for 'more professional', you take the good bits from industry such as greater efficiency and adaptability, but not the ruthlessness of Dark Corporation. In industry you introduce compassion where it's missing, or develop a business model that demonstrates true responsibility for Life.

Maybe in your spare time you work for free on projects you really care about. If you're officially retired, and you want the rest of your life to be useful as well as enjoyable, perhaps you play the Altruist avatar by volunteering your time and energy. You find out who needs what in your community, or use a website like Do-it. Or maybe you make beautiful things, or share your knowledge, experience and wisdom with those younger than you.

Playing Altruist, you do the work you do primarily because you care about the outcomes (although getting paid is useful too). Whether your work is law or lavatory cleaning, you're playing Altruist when you do it in a way that scores for Life.

If you're unemployed, you're trying to find work that will be good for you and for the world – though Dark State insists you can't be fussy. You send your CV to, or talk to, organisations working for something you care about. You want an employer who genuinely takes social and environmental responsibility seriously. Though in an increasingly tough society, you might be so desperate that any paid work will do – your first concern for Life is first to make sure your own needs are met. You score for Life when you qualify as a youth worker, for example, despite all the obstacles in your way. You're playing Hero when you're active in dissolving the obstacles that prevent players doing the good work they're capable of.

You can also support Life by challenging damaging work around the world: sign petitions, write emails, share on social media. You can shop for Life, supporting local businesses and traders trying to do good work that they love. You can buy locally grown, made and sold whenever possible. That way you become part of the community – which might well lead to your own venture, so that you too can enjoy doing what you're best at.

You play Hero in this field when you take risks or make sacrifices to help work serve Life. Maybe you're persuaded a global organisation such as Kingfisher, PepsiCo or Unilever to become as sustainable as possible. Perhaps you work for a charity, using your skills for Life even though the salary is half what it might be with an employer engaged in destructive activities. Or you're active in a trade union, defending players who might otherwise be financially or emotionally crushed by the Dark Powers.

You might play Hero by experimenting with new working models. The Mondragon Corporation, founded in the Basque region of Spain in the 1950s, was a Heroic forerunner of workers' co-operatives. The business has experimented over various sectors with democratic and Life-enhancing forms of collaboration, and its model of social justice and environmental responsibility has spread worldwide (although not without hiccups). In Yorkshire, Suma Wholefoods is a worker's co-operative scoring for Life. Suma pays all its members the same hourly rate, and everyone participates in decision-making. Its product range is based around health, animal welfare, fair trade and environmental responsibility. Riverford Organics is following the same path.

Self-employment, social enterprises and ethical businesses of any size offer the best opportunities for good work. But in any job there are ways to score for Life, and they all help drive out the Dark Powers out of the workplace.

State of Play
The Dark Powers currently dominate the working world. We need the energy of the unemployed, communication skills from marketing and media, strategy and application from the military, cash from the financial sector, practical skills from construction, to create a healthy future: planting trees, educating for wellbeing, developing energy technologies, helping displaced people, cleaning up the ocean. Most work that scores for Life is done by volunteers; it could be the basis of our economy.

Resources for Life

Book: *The Power of Just Doing Stuff*, Rob Hopkins

Book: *Future Fit,* Giles Hutchins

Book: *Holonomics,* Simon & Maria Robinson

Book: *Postcapitalism – A Guide to our Future*

Book: *Hearing our Calling,* Gill Coombs

Film: The Corporation

Film: Own the Change

YouTube: Your Lifestyle Has Already Been Designed

TED talk: The 21 hour work week, Anna Coote

REconomy.org

Transition.org

Businessgreen.com

Greenjobs.co.uk

Charityjob.co.uk

Do-it.org

Field 6: Health

In this Game, you only get one life. We generally come into the Game with everything we need for health, but gradually the Dark Powers (and occasional random misfortune) erode our health. Your miraculously clever body works constantly to balance, detoxify and repair itself, to maintain a state of health. Helping it, you score for Life. The more aware you are, the easier this is.

THE DARK POWERS

The Dark Powers play the Game in the Health field by scoring from illness and suffering. Collectively, they benefit from poor physical and mental health created by the activities of the Dark Powers. Some believe this is a very deliberate strategy of individual Manipulator avatars; others say that's a conspiracy theory.

Either way, it's easy to see how such a system self-perpetuates. Rather than address some of the less direct but most pervasive root causes of sickness in society such as poor diet, poverty and a stressful work and entertainment culture, those in power allow them to proliferate. Players are encouraged to medicate, and healthcare costs soar. Most drugs have side effects as well as positive effects, and some unfortunate players find themselves bound to a lifetime feedback loop of poor health and medication.

Damage to Life is caused in the overlap between the Health and Money fields, where the value of Life itself is measured in terms of cost and efficiency. You might say this is the 'real world', but money dominates healthcare rather than supports it is that the world you want?

Manipulators might run big pharmaceutical companies, making a fortune through a monopoly over drugs or medical equipment. Some play Cynic designing or promoting meds that counteract the side effects of other meds – knowing there are natural, but less lucrative, solutions. Certain academics have been known to receive financial or other incentives from the pharmaceutical industry for promoting certain drugs or vaccines in teaching or research. They have some very wealthy and powerful Manipulators behind them: anyone who challenges the safety of those drugs too publicly can be dragged through the courts, or bought out.

Sleepwalking or Cynical shareholders push for their pharmaceutical company to become ever more profitable. This can be achieved by making medicines extremely expensive – not because they're costly to produce, but because they're unique, so the drugs company names their price. This costs the NHS a fortune: all the more for Cynical shareholders.

Synthetic foodstuffs and environmental toxins cause many of our physical health problems. Breakdown of community, rigorous testing at school, stressful work, debt, violent and dysfunction TV, computer games and internet content, alienation from the natural world, and the self-medication of alcohol (a known depressant) all contribute to mental health issues. The Dark Powers in all of us are responsible for this damage, and those playing Manipulator profit from it. Their own expensive healthcare is sophisticated, comfortable and immediate.

You have to play the Cynic to install hospital vending machines that sell fatty, salty, and sugary snacks, and stock carbonated drinks that leach calcium from bones. Often renting space outside cardiac units or near the osteoporosis clinic, these enterprises are all about money and nothing about nutrition.

Private recruitment agencies also make a fortune from the NHS by recruiting poorly paid nurses from other countries – caring nothing for the nurses or their patients; only profit. (If you recruit nurses primarily to meet desperate need in healthcare, you're playing Altruist.)

The Dark Powers have crushed Life through the Duty of Care culture that profits from a community so fractured, that care no longer just happens naturally. 'Ambulance-chasing' law firms use aggressive direct marketing to persuade accident victims to sue for damages.

Some play Cynic in their involvement with outsourcing healthcare and related services. Busy negotiating lucrative contracts, they have little interest in all those workers who get up every day hoping to make life easier for the people in their care, or for their worried families. The focus is on buyouts, balance sheets and shareholders.

Orchestrating privatisation of the NHS, Manipulator and Cynic avatars strike deals benefiting companies in which they or their family have financial interests. Some play the Cynic as hypocritical politicians: saying all the right things about the NHS to help them win votes, but reneging once in power. The Dark Powers are constantly in and out of the revolving door that has lucrative healthcare contracts in equipment, medication, IT, or other services on one side – and influential government roles on the other. In fact, they keep it turning.

But in the Health field, most players are trying to score for Life.

HOW TO SCORE FOR LIFE

We all know the timeless essentials for health: good food, enough exercise and rest, a degree of cleanliness, and general emotional wellbeing.

For the good of Life you need to be fully aware of the Dark Powers' current threats to your health: polluted air, synthetic chemical compounds and refined sugar in food; a daily life of sitting; hormone-disrupting make-up and creams absorbed by your body; toxic solvents and formaldehyde in a new home, office or car. These are some of the health traps Dark Corporation have lied about to score in the Game; traps you need to avoid in order to stay healthy. For example, you might buy a replacement sofa every few years, unaware that the flame retardant it's sprayed with contains a toxin that can affect your brain. You might be equally astonished to find your pillows have also been dipped in neuro-toxins.

When you first become aware of all these threats to Health it can be overwhelming, flipping you into Avoider (where you carry on as if the threats weren't real). But you can take back control of what enters your body: there are toxin-free versions of just about everything you can buy. Any changes you make to your home environment are of course optional, and as gradual or swift as you want them to be.

You score for Life when you look after your body, enjoying the sense of vitality that courses through you when you're well and fit. And when you do become ill, you're fending off the Dark Powers if you're able to appreciate, maintain and improve the health you do have; not always easy. Playing Altruist, you know you're a unique expression of Life: one that you have the pleasure of – and the ultimate responsibility for.

You win in this field when you help your body keep in balance through plenty of movement, whether walking, dancing, gardening or more formal exercise, which all lead to healthier body and mind. When your body's tired, you work your mind; when your mind's tired you work your body. And when mind, body and soul are all tired, you rest: properly, and for as long as it takes.

You do your best to avoid toxins in the air, your food, or your home and furniture – not only because toxins can badly damage your awareness. You eat well, remembering also to feed the community of bacteria in your gut that help preserve your emotional wellbeing. Maybe you cut alcohol out, or have it as an occasional treat. When you take this step you are probably delighted by the improvement to your physical and mental health – the older you are, the more you'll notice this.

You know your mind affects your body, just as your body affects your mind. So for physical wellbeing you look after your emotional life: practising self-awareness, self-acceptance, mindfulness and healthy emotions such as gratitude, compassion and acceptance. All this can take discipline, especially if you're too strict with yourself. You can't do super-healthy things 24/7, and that's okay; any positive thing you do for your health scores for Life. And remember, collaboration can help wonderfully: in the form of teachers, therapists, community or friends. All you have to do is reach out till you connect. And you will.

If you're a parent, you naturally want your children to grow up healthy and happy, full of Life. So playing Altruist instead of Sleepwalker or Avoider, you spend time outdoors with them, protect them from toxic environments, and nourish their bodies (and emotional life) as well as you can. You collaborate rather than compete with other parents: there is an old saying that 'it takes a whole village to raise a child'. In the Altruist avatar you also notice and help any other players who are struggling, scoring for Life by acting for the health of the greater good.

When your body goes wrong, you can help Life by trying natural healing methods first, or products without harmful side effects; not dangerous to animals or environment in their testing, production and disposal. (However, it's worth remembering that the Altruist avatar could be led, through its natural idealism, to a practise or product that's untried and potentially harmful.)

When things go wrong with your mind, it can be deeply distressing. But in the Sleepwalker avatar you're at risk of accepting medication of mental illness as a societal norm. You may not know that turbulent phases naturally occur throughout life – and that properly supported within community, they can be important times of growth. This knowledge has been lost in today's world. Instead you take advice, maybe from of a kind Traditionalist who's disturbed by something that seems out of control.

You accept the notion of 'normal' that insists something is fundamentally wrong with you, and needs to be put right. (Although sometimes, of course, the right medication can save your life.)

Maybe you're a habitual Traditionalist who's never dreamt of going to an 'alternative' practitioner using herbal treatments, or acupuncture. Even though these treatments are traditional and modern medicine is a relatively new invention, you might trust the authority figures who say state-backed medicine is the only model that's reliable. Everything else is unscientific and to be viewed with great suspicion. But eventually, you could be in so much pain that you move out of your habitual avatar for long enough to try yoga, for example. It might relieve your joint pain almost immediately, and change your view permanently!

If you play the Altruist avatar at work in the health sector, you're in your job primarily because you care about others and genuinely want to alleviate suffering – or even better, prevent it. You might, as a healthcare professional, witness unethical practices: whether cutting corners in patient care, or dubious use of funds. You could choose to play the Hero avatar and speak out, maybe risking being bullied by colleagues or losing your job. Finding others on the side of Life can really help here. And if you do succeed, the damage of the Dark Powers is diminished.

You might score for Life in research, or working for a major drugs company, because your passion is developing effective new medicines or big picture strategies for wellbeing. You might play Hero as a health expert seeking to work with government, lobbying for legislation about unhealthy food. Or perhaps you prefer a political role, attempting to address mental health issues by treating them as a serious symptom of societal factors.

Maybe you work in a surgery, and you can see ways how patient care could be improved. You might feel overwhelmed by the sheer weight of the system that you feel helpless, but for Life's sake you try to make a difference anyway. Or maybe you benefit Life outside the system:

bringing skills of healing, whether acupuncture or chiropractor; herbalist or chiropodist.

Maybe you played Hero by striking in support of Junior Doctors, helping them hold a line between their work for Life and the forced impositions of Dark State. Maybe you are one of those Junior Doctors, who took public flak (incited by Dark Media) for holding out. But if you don't care about anyone who suffered through the strike, and were just looking out for your own needs, you were playing Cynic.

Some score for Life developing new medical technology, working on projects such as GSK and Veriliy's bio-electronic medical treatment. You could develop a new drug that saves millions of lives, risking years of dedication to something that might not work. (When you save millions of lives, paradoxically you're also putting great strain on Life itself, facilitating the growth of the species that causes the most destruction. We know – it's complex.)

The Red Cross are national and international Health Heroes. The doctors of *Médecins Sans Frontières* also go wherever need is greatest. Individual Heroes volunteer to work in some of the most dangerous places: communities ravaged by Ebola, refugee camps in Europe, devastated cities in Syria. A poignant YouTube video shows CCTV footage of one the last paediatricians in Aleppo, beginning his shift just before he was killed by a Russian air strike.

But when someone like philanthropic capitalist Richard Branson negotiates lucrative deals with the NHS to run its hospitals through 'Virgin Care', it can be hard for other players to tell whether he's playing Hero or Manipulator – or both. It's possible to play Manipulator and Hero simultaneously: take wellbeing gurus who encourage others to depend on them, attracting wealth, power and prestige whilst helping people improve their lives.

The NHS is of course the UK's national Health Hero, with its massive daily contribution to Life. The NHS is vast, unwieldy and imperfect. But it provides free healthcare to all, and employs hundreds of thousands who step into Hero every day, doing their best despite a chronic shortage of funding and resources. You might play Hero in your work as a nurse, paramedic, doctor, specialist, auxiliary or volunteer. A dedicated carer or healer, you do what you can in a depleted, stretched and bureaucratic system.

Compassion and care can get lost in a culture of targets, efficiency budgets, and risk avoidance. But in Hero, you do your best for sick and wounded people who might be having the worst day of their Life. You're physically and emotionally exhausted at the end of a long shift. You might not blame colleagues who leave due to poor conditions, or burnout. But you stay on to make a difference, and Life is stronger as a result.

State of Play

This is a field full of players in Altruist and Hero, doing amazing work for Life. Most work they do is combating the side effects of activities of the Dark Powers, and Manipulator and Cynic avatars make their work more difficult by profitising healthcare. Life is holding its ground but we desperately need strategic Game changes. If fields such as Food and Work can be won for Life, Health will follow naturally.

Resources for Life

Book: *Freakonomics*
Film/Game: Big Pharma
Magazine: Natural Health
Facebook: Ayurveda
Facebook: Healthy Holistic Living
Mindbodyspirit.co.uk
Naturalhealth.co.uk
NHSonline.org
Redcross.org.uk
Explorehealthyfood.com
MSF.org.uk
Naturalnews.com

Field 7: Food

Food is a huge part of our lives, and not just because we love it. Food is one of the most important fields because *you are what you eat*. Everything you take into your body *becomes* your body, and affects your mind-state too. Every time you eat or drink, you score for Life or the Dark Powers by how it affects you, and also how it's grown and transported. It's good we can choose how to play this field.

THE DARK POWERS

Every Player needs to eat, so the opportunities for domination and exploitation in this field are limitless.

In the Food field, the Dark Powers move to control anything that can be commodified. They command extraction and sale of spring water from drought areas, scheme to convince mothers that synthetic baby food is better than breast milk, and endorse slave labour on cocoa farms. They orchestrate global transportation of food that could be grown and eaten locally. Efficiency of scale swells their profits, but ruins farmers and small manufacturers, and sucks money out of local economies.

The Dark Powers run global Food conglomerates. Their main concern is maximising profit for shareholders. Although they're in the food business they have little or no interest in nutrition or wellbeing. In fact some instruct lawyers to sue governments for insisting on honest labelling (in countries that have signed a trade agreement allowing this).

Buyers negotiate Dark Corporation contracts with banana growers or dairy farmers that leave them barely able to scratch a living, and under permanent threat of losing their contract, despite long hours of hard and skilful work. Cynic avatars set company policies that reject vast amounts of good food, because its shape isn't regular enough for the perfect image that Dark Corporation would have players believe is normal. And yet... you might play Cynic in the food field just to make a living, whilst playing Hero in another (or even the same) field at the same time.

When a certain foodstuff is in demand (usually because players believed the marketing hype), Manipulators arrange for it to be produced in vast quantities – even when the necessary land-grabbing results in people and other creatures losing their homes, destruction of ecosystems, extinction of species, and threats to biodiversity.

The Dark Powers permeate global seed companies, forcing farmers into dependency by making it *illegal* (with Dark State's help) *to save seed from their own crops.* Patenting vegetables potentially gives Manipulators exclusive ownership. Perhaps their ultimate aim is to patent Life...

Dark Corporation sells processed food to players as a quick win. (In an overlap with the work field, many don't have the time to cook because of long hours, or the energy to cook because of being stressed and tired.) Dark Corporation don't mention that processed food usually contains refined sugars, unhealthy fats, hidden ingredients, and a dazzling spectrum of artificial chemicals; fruit and veg soaked in pesticides and herbicides, processed meat from animals or fish stuffed with hormones and antibiotics. They don't mention the link between a sharp rise in diabetes, cancer, heart disease and mental health issues, and the rise of highly processed diets.

Someone was playing Cynic in this field when they came up with the idea of sawdust to bulk out biscuits, or artificial additives that make food look fresh when it's not. So are scientists, who agree, for large sums of money, to publish 'findings' that a certain product is good for health, or that certain chemical additives aren't harmful.

Dark State allows Dark Corporation to literally poison players with chemical-laden 'goods', instead of supporting organic growers rather than giant agriculture, and giving all players better access to delicious, nutritious food – which you might expect from leaders genuinely concerned about the health and wellbeing of the population (after all, what is actually more important than that?). Most supermarket bosses dictate a strategy that builds in waste, so they can keep their shelves as full as the competition. Food ends up in the skip, while players struggle to afford to eat.

The Dark Powers also run industrial scale piggeries or fisheries, hardened to the suffering of billions of beings so they can churn out high volume 'produce'. They farm vast acres of monocrop cereal on starved soil, sprayed with pesticides that kill bees. They take government subsidies for large scale agriculture and say they're 'feeding the world', when permaculture technology can produce more food per acre *and* benefit Life at the same time.

Technically, there's no need for anyone to play Manipulator or hard Cynic avatars in this field. Good food can be both profitable and affordable, creating a healthy economy with good jobs… but not when the Dark Powers make food into something cheap and exploitative.

HOW TO SCORE FOR LIFE

This is a field where players love scoring for Life: whether the satisfaction of growing and preparing food, the shared joy of cooking and eating with others, the sensory delights of eating good quality food, however basic – or making a living from this field in some way.

If you've been Sleepwalking, your avatar is likely to morph once you know about the relationship between the Dark Powers and Food. You might move to Avoider: knowing, but not willing to eat differently. Or you might live with your food choices for now, not giving yourself a hard time while you consider changes. Who knows: you might choose to move straight into Altruist or Hero, and begin a new relationship with food right away. This happens to lots of players.

Likely you had no idea what's gone into producing food on the supermarket shelf: who's profited and who's suffered. The labels tell a happy story that you accepted without thinking about it. And you're not to blame; you always assumed someone was taking care of such things. Isn't that what we have governments for? But once you see behind the marketing veil, you might decide to get whatever you can from ethical and local suppliers. You check out (or just avoid) vague ingredients such as 'preservatives', knowing they could include butylated hydroxytoluene, and other possible cancer-causing synthetic chemicals. ('Natural colourings' can legally include some metals.)

To score for Life you can avoid supermarkets altogether – particularly if you're concerned about where the Food field overlaps with the fields of Community, Animals and Planet Earth. Instead you use farm shops, local stores, or online organic supplier such as Riverford or Abel and Cole (who are not perfect, but base their business on scoring for Life). You eat seasonally: reducing food miles as well as having everything fresh, which is so much better for taste and texture, as well as your body. If money is tight, only you can decide what takes priority over food.

With greater awareness, you no longer just buy whatever fish you fancy, but check whether it's a species that's abundant, or on the edge of extinction. You now know that orang-utans are dying in forests cleared for palm oil – which you didn't realise was in your chocolate bar or margarine. You find yourself considering the daily life of the pig now neatly divided into Styrofoam-packed chops. Before, it didn't even occur to you: a carefully chosen image made you think of farms, and the outdoors, and health.

With all the advertising pushing quick, cheap food, you probably thought you didn't have enough time or money for decent meals. But one day you realise you truly deserve better – and can have better. You eat as well as you can, even if you don't have much spare cash and can't afford organic (which shouldn't cost more, but does because of Dark Corporation). You know what's in everything you eat – real Food doesn't have many ingredients – and usually where it's come from. You get your veg from local growers who don't spray chemicals, even if they don't have time to jump through all the hoops of being certified organic. You could even forage, eating for free most of the year from the wild edibles that are abundant in fields, hedgerows, seashores or even your own back garden.

You can score for bigtime for Life growing your own, even in a small garden. You can get a veg box from a country or city farm, and cook from scratch. For tinned and dried stuff there's affordable real food from wholesalers such as Suma or Essential; you could buy in bulk with friends, direct from them online. Maybe you just eat less – and discover you actually feel better. Maybe, no longer in a binge and despair cycle, you post more images of delicious meals that score for Life on Instagram than pics of booze, crisps, chocolate or ice cream frenzies.

When you move out of Avoider, you no longer fancy baby sweetcorn, pork escallops, Belgian chocolates or cheese biscuits for your dinner party, having fact-checked about air miles, intensive farming, slave labour and plastic packaging. In the Altruist avatar, you understand the devastating impact of plastics on wildlife, soil, and the ocean, so you take your own bags and buy food with little or no packaging.

You could to score for Life by selling or serving good food. You might grow veg, fruit, nut trees, salad leaves or even just herbs for family and friends, or for sale. You may not be officially organic, but you use few or no artificial chemicals. You grow in a way that enhances rather than depletes the soil – that vital substance from which all our food comes. And you save your precious seeds for next year.

You might score for Life as a vegan, if you believe a meat diet is environmentally destructive, or don't want to exploit animals for their milk, eggs and other products. Or you might be vegetarian, if you can justify a bit of exploitation but don't want to be responsible for taking a sentient being's life. If you do eat meat or dairy products, you score for Life when you make sure they come from high welfare farms, ideally where animal rearing is integrated with the landscape and nature, benefiting the Life in soil.

If you've been playing the Traditionalist avatar, you might have fully trusted institutions like the National Farmers Union. But you no longer accept that if the NFU says we have to kill badgers, or spray herbicides, or grow insect-resistant GMOs, then we do. You fact-check. And you find that bovine TB is caused by modern dairy farming practises and inflicted on badgers by humans, and that 'organic wholefoods' are actually traditional rather than alternative: what everyone ate before highly processed food was invented in the 20th century.

Scoring for Life, you waste nothing. Sell-by dates are generally a Cynical tool to avoid being sued, and don't define the actual state of the food item. You trust smell-by dates more than sell-by dates. That way you don't consign a perfectly good jar of marmalade to the bin, or eat mozzarella that's still in date if your nose tells you it's off.

With awareness, you know how wonderful and vital real food is; what it contributes to the Life flowing through your body. You eat with gratitude, especially after a purging fast. You know what foods work best with your body, and what to avoid. (If you indulge each latest super-food or intolerance on a whim, you're actually playing Sleepwalker.) Sometimes you indulge yourself with a technically unhealthy, but nevertheless delicious, treat. As professional caterer and blogger Tara Vaughan-Hughes points out, enjoying your food is the most important thing. If you start from a healthy base, a little bit of what you fancy will do you more good than harm.

Hugh Fearnley-Whittingstall is a well-known food Hero, getting important truths about intensive fishing and farming out to other players on prime time TV. And Jamie Oliver, love him or hate him, has turned the Game around in school canteens. Another food warrior is Vandana Shiva, calmly challenging seed giant Monsanto, protecting food rights in India and across the world. The small farmers bringing legal action against powerful Monsanto are also playing the Hero avatar.

The Fair Trade organisation has long played collective Hero, ensuring people and land are not exploited through production of commodities such as coffee, chocolate, bananas and much more. Some towns have collectively played the Hero avatar, declaring themselves a Fair Trade town. But recently Fair Trade has come under attack from some as being infiltrated by the Dark Powers, and other organisations with the same aims, such as Fair for Life, are springing up.

Most organic farmers play Hero: it takes Courage to farm this way in a competitive world bent on cost-cutting. However some play Cynic, farming organically by the book, but not in spirit. With no real love of animals or the land, they cut ethical corners wherever possible, with an eye on premium prices. But they're scoring for Life anyway as they benefit soil, wildlife and people. And all the time, new growers are stepping into the Hero avatar, farming for Life. Heroes nationwide are pushing for organic produce not to require certification, instead for 'conventional' food to detail the chemicals used to produce it.

Anyone who's fighting for laws that would make decent Food available to everyone at an affordable price is playing Hero. The current system favours supermarkets and global conglomerates; the solutions are complex, but possible and viable with the right intention.

You could be a Hero engaging in 'guerrilla gardening' (planting edibles in public spaces). Or you could take up skipping: retrieving discarded Food from supermarket skips, for those who have little or nothing to eat.

Other ways of scoring for Life in this field include designing apps to help players manage food consumption, and conducting academic studies of food poverty.

It can take courage to ask questions about provenance and animal welfare standards, but doing so scores for Life, letting retailers or caterers know players care. That can change their purchasing policies: never underestimate the power of the purse. Asking the question might feel uncomfortable, especially if you walk away when the answer isn't good. That's why it puts you in Hero.

State of Play

Because all players are guaranteed to spend money on food, it's riddled with Manipulators looking to profit from our need to eat. But recently Life has made massive gains on the Dark Powers. Provenance has become a mainstream issue. There are many passionate players doing good work in this field. But we still have far too many players in Sleepwalker, trustingly eating what they are sold by Dark Corporation.

Book: *In Defence of Food: an Eater's Manifesto*, Michael Pollan

Radio: *The Food Programme*, Radio 4

Film: *Food, Inc*. Robert Kenner

Magazine: *The Land*

Facebook: Wild Food UK

Thevillagefarm.co.uk

Sustainablefoodtrust.org

Riverford.org

Abelandcole.co.uk

Suma.coop

Essential-trading.co.uk

Fairtrade.org.uk

Verticalveg.org.uk

Permaculture.org.uk

Landworkersalliance.org.uk

Field 8: Stuff

Most players love to shop: a day out at a retail park, or hours browsing online. But without awareness, shopping for stuff scores for the Dark Powers. The global economy is based on mass production and consumption of stuff, but with just one planet this clearly isn't going to work for long. The stuff we buy plays a huge part in shaping not only our lives, but the future of Life itself.

THE DARK POWERS

The Manipulator avatar sees the world as a giant commodity, people as consumers and other living beings as expendable. Land and ocean are exploited; indigenous people and creatures suffer and die – but they weren't buying stuff, so their lives don't matter to the Dark Powers.

The Dark Powers depend on players buying stuff: the more, the better. Most of their production systems use synthetic chemicals that end up in the environment, and burn fossil fuels that push climate change towards a fatal tipping point. There are toxic lakes of pollution from the factories of Chinese electronics giant Foxconn; suicide nets over the windows of their workers' dormitories – and Sleepwalkers buying their products every day.

People playing Manipulator might own a giant fashion company, beauty industry, or car manufacturer, or run an enormous retail group like British Home Stores.

Dark Corporation grooms politicians, persuading those in government that economic growth based on extraction and fossil fuels really is healthy rather than fatal. They manoeuvre for binding trade agreements so they will be able to sue any government which legislates to protect people, animals or land. They swallow up pristine wild habitats. and suck the souls out of countless workers to fund their luxurious lives, and throw titbits to the rest of us in the form of designer labels.

Hard Cynics are willing tools of the big boys and girls, implementing the master plan of extract, make and sell. They display designer labels to help them get ahead. Some play Cynic using their degree in art or psychology not to score for Life, as they could, but to coerce players into spending. They use 'greenwash' to suck trusting players from Altruist into Sleepwalker: rustic colours, rural scenes and words such as 'natural' and 'sustainable': language and images properly used in service of Life, stolen and corrupted by the Dark Powers.

Cynic avatars lobby politicians and force through land grabs. Hard Cynics arrange the deaths of inconvenient players like Honduras business woman and activist Lesbia Yaneth Urquía, who publicly opposed privatisation of natural resources for corporate gain.

Cambodia is one of several countries where factory workers make branded clothes for players in wealthier countries. When they protest peacefully for a living wage they are shot, beaten and controlled by armed, visored forces: Cynical, Traditionalist or Sleepwalking tools of collusion between Dark Corporation and Dark State.

You're Sleepwalking when you buy these clothes made from synthetic materials by children 'somewhere overseas', clothes you'll throw away in a year because they've lost their shape or gone out of fashion – even though they'll probably be on trend again in a few years.

Cynics make cars that deliberately cheat emissions tests, or design and market goods with 'built in obsolescence'. So when other players buy light bulbs, clothes, washing machines, phones or tablets, they will soon have to ditch them because of *a fault designed into the product*. This is a top scorer for the Dark Powers. In Sleepwalker you accept built-in obsolescence: when things go wrong, you throw them away and buy another (if you can afford to) without question. After all, they're cheap. Get stuff repaired? That's what your grandad did. You buy new stuff before the old stuff has even reached landfill.

Playing the Avoider avatar, you recognise that okay, you probably do have too many clothes. But when you're invited to a party, you scan the wardrobe, imagining what other people will be wearing. You have a quick look online, and before long there's a nice big parcel arriving by courier. You do feel bad about the sheer amount of stuff you buy. But the family expects a certain standard of living, and if you don't keep up with that standard you'll have failed. The Dark Powers understand and target your fear; after all, they created it.

When you're Sleepwalking in this field, Dark Corporation get their stuff deep under your skin every hour of the day. They sneak in through online ads, on TV, in shop windows, by the road, in magazines, at sports events. They manipulate you with images of what you should look like, what you should have, what your life should be. They understand and play on your desires, dreams and insecurities. Dark Corporation sells you stuff to make you feel better about the harm they've done to you in the fields of work or community. Possessions become symbolic of your self-worth, replacing all the natural, Life-enhancing things you could so easily have and be.

You're scoring for the Dark Powers from a Sleepwalker or Traditionalist avatar when you think it's fine to give kids so many presents that they just glance at most of them and throw them to one side; when they have piles of plastic toys that lie unused around the garden until they find their way to landfill. There can be joy without plastic. It's ironic that handcrafted toys from natural materials are often called 'traditional', and yet the Traditionalist avatar sees them as 'alternative' or even sneers at them for being handmade. And of course children want the toys they've seen on TV.

You might call someone who raises objections a 'killjoy', and perhaps you're right. But that doesn't mean the problems aren't real: not only the damage done in the toys' making and disposal, but the lasting lessons children learn about value, gratitude and respect.

Some Cynics' prime market is children, but advertisers cynically appeal to the child in all of us with innocent plinky tunes, animated characters with big eyes, cute animals, or a phrase like 'We Care'. Who cares whether what they're selling does good or harm? Not them. They only care that it sells.

Do you remember thinking marketing directly to children was wrong when it started? Now it just seems normal. The more players Dark Corporation can suck into the Sleepwalker avatar at a young age, the more their vision of a consumer world comes true. They spend billions on advertising, to keep you and as many players shopping as much as possible.

And shop you do, when you're playing Sleepwalker – whether you can afford it or not: games and apps because they're new, insecure networked devices because they're cool, cars and furniture because they're 'aspirational'. Stuff for your baby, your pets, kitchen, car, and garden; and specialised stuff for every single activity you can think of, including sex. Do you need all this stuff? That's not even a question.

Until you realise you've been had.

HOW TO SCORE FOR LIFE

When you decide to start scoring for Life in the field of Stuff, the first thing you do is buy less stuff. You only get what you need, or what brings lasting pleasure. But some players love shopping. They enjoy not only what they buy, but the pleasure of shopping with others. Luckily, not all shopping is harmful. It only serves the Dark Powers when products do harm in their making, packaging, use or disposal, or when money goes to big corporations. It's quite possible to buy Stuff and score for Life at the same time!

Maybe you've been playing the Traditionalist avatar, trusting brands that have been around all your life, and longer. Familiar names like The Co-operative, Land Rover and Hotpoint, with their reputation for quality, feel safe – and Cynical marketers know that. That's why they kept the name, long after the original firm, location and business model were replaced by a profit-hungry transnational corporation. But after some fact-checking, you've had to acknowledge that these brands are simply no longer as ethical or reliable.

Maybe you become aware that you've been pouring acid, phosphates, plastic microbeads, and oestrogen down your drains and eventually into the waterways. You do a bit of research, and realise you don't need Dark Corporation's powerful cleaning products and toiletries. You no longer flush tampons, cleansing pads or cotton buds down the toilet to cause harm in rivers and oceans.

Waking up from the Sleepwalker avatar, you realise you don't need disposable stuff to make parties and weddings attractive. Subtle but powerful marketing taught you to stay childlike in your desire for pretty things, but it's as if a part of you has grown up: learnt that pleasures can have unintended consequences.

Playing the Altruist avatar, you assess scores for Life and the Dark Powers with each purchase. When you start it can be tedious, and hard to calculate. You seem to spend your life doing research and asking for recommendations from other players. But eventually you reach a point when you know which toiletries, cleaning products, clothes, make-up, cards, gifts, books, furniture and toys score highest. You know where to get recyclable dishcloths and felt mobile covers, and you share sources on social media. You use a mooncup instead of tampons, and get take-out coffee in your own mug.

To score for Life you buy the best quality things you can afford because they will last a really long time, and will not harm your health or your family's. You avoid packaging as much as possible, *particularly if it's plastic*. Maybe you declutter, keeping only what you consider useful, beautiful, or a precious reminder of people or times gone by. With less Stuff you feel lighter, as if you'd done a detox or a juice cleanse: it brings you back to Life.

You mend appliances, look after tools, and don't wash clothes as often. You learn that cotton – water-thirsty and drenched in insecticides – is one of the most damaging crops on earth, so you get your clothes from charity shops, or buy items made of bamboo or hemp for their lower environmental impact; after all, they look and feel just as nice.

When you do part with things, they go to a charity shop or on Freecycle rather than landfill. And you get stuff from charity shops, jumble trails, Gumtree, eBay or Freecycle, or swapping with friends. This scores hugely for Life by cutting out the manufacture and disposal of every new item you don't buy. Also you save money, and maybe help a charity. If you want new stuff, you get it from local makers or independent stores, putting money back into the local economy and getting to know your community, bringing Life into places that had the soul sucked out of them by The Dark Powers.

If you can't get what you want locally there are ethical online stores, or Etsy's site for cottage industry handmade goods. You discover that handmade goods are usually far better quality and more beautiful than mass-produced factory line objects.

You can score for Life making things for pleasure, putting love for the recipient into cards or gifts. You don't worry about them not looking 'professional' – they're real. You enjoy receiving a unique card or gift; something that expresses the giver's personality, that did no harm in its making, and is higher quality than mass-produced stuff. If you don't have the time or inclination to make something, you support someone else by buying theirs. Sometimes it takes discipline, when it would be easier to pop into the corner shop, but on the whole you find it's worth it.

Some players aren't into making things, but more into communication. The Stuff culture keeps so many players asleep that you could make it your mission to score in this field by helping to wake them up.

When you're trying to score for Life, you might fall for Dark Corporation's 'greenwash' and buy products marketed with wholesome words like 'harvest' and pictures of a healthy planet, without fact-checking. Or you might fall into the trap of buying cynically marketed 'spirituality accessories'. Cynical marketers know that some Altruists are a little naïve, and convince them they're spending ethically when they're not. At such times habitual Altruists are actually Sleepwalking.

No-one can play the Altruist avatar all the time. But with practise you find it's possible to live quite happily for long stretches without buying online from a big corporate; even without stepping into a supermarket, retail park or chain store. Eventually, these places feel artificial and bizarre.

Heroes in the field of stuff follow the money and challenge the Manipulators gobbling up players and Planet. Campaigner Annie Leonard made the classic animation Story of Stuff, which shows exactly how the extraction-pollution-exploitation-production-consumption-ejection cycle works. The project continues to add animations to its website from the Story of Electronics to the Story of Microbeads, and has an active Facebook page.

In the US, stuff Hero Jo Stodgel runs Upcycle Santa Fe. He takes plastic packaging and turns it into treasure, using it to make items such as jewellery, and eco-bricks that can be used for construction. Beth Terry, an accountant from California, was so shocked when she found out about the impact of plastics on wildlife that she started a personal plastic-free challenge that went viral. Meanwhile in China, Mr Li has made more than six thousand musical instruments from trash. All over the world people are playing Stuff Hero: whether making organic cleaning products, or 'repurposing' sandals from discarded fishing nets.

There are plenty of ways to play the Hero avatar in this field. If you make things, you could start a business teaching others. Or you could be the one working in big business with the courage to suggest and drive through a recyclable packaging policy, or the one who shoulders the risk of switching to more expensive organic cotton.

You could play Hero by starting a Library of Things. What's the point of everyone in a community owning a tent, a sack truck or a cake icing kit, when they're only used once or twice a year? Far better to collectively own a few of these items, for people to take out when they need them. It builds strong community networks too, which scores bonus points for Life.

State of Play
The Dark Powers could win the Game through this field. The culture of Stuff is extinguishing Life on the land and in the oceans. Manufacture, transport and disposal of Stuff are driving spiraling climate changes that could extinguish Life as we know it. Players in Manipulator and hard Cynic keep other players dependent on Stuff, and Heroes can't do much to change that. Only through Sleepwalkers waking up can Life reclaim this field.

Resources for Life

Book: *A Handmade Life*, William Coperthwaite
Book: *Green Cleaning*, Margaret Briggs
Film: *The True Cost*
YouTube: Labour behind the Label
YouTube: The Story of Stuff
Storyofstuff.org
Ethicalconsumer.org
Myplasticfreelife.com
Freecycle.org

Gumtree.com
Libraryofthings.co.uk
Braintreeclothing.com
Bambooclothing.co.uk
Komodo.co.uk
Etsy.com

Field 9: Politics

Politics is the field that determines how the rest of the Game is run: what the rules are; who can do what. As you'd expect, you'll find plenty of Manipulator avatars in Politics. But you'll also find Heroes. In this field, epic struggles between Life and the Dark Powers are played out. The outcomes affect all fields, and are central to the outcome of the Game.

THE DARK POWERS

The struggle between Life and the Dark Powers has been playing out in the politics field for everyone to see.

Manipulators have not only been unmasked, but have declared themselves blatantly. It's telling that so many players in the UK, Europe and the States have been choosing candidates so clearly on the side of the Dark Powers. As in the playground, a lot identify with the winning side as they see those playing Hero rubbished, pulled apart or simply ignored. It's primal stuff. Dark State and Dark Media have played their game very effectively.

Many players are in stunned disbelief: how could things have come to this? Whilst so many were Sleepwalking, the Dark Powers have moved swiftly ahead, and this field is in chaos.

In politics, everyone claims to be on the side of Life, and many politicians believe themselves to be. But some enter the field with no other goal than power and influence. They grew up as part of an elite group like The Riot Club (a film based on the real Bullingdon Club) which gave them a sense of entitlement, hedonism, and power. The top slice of society is the only one they know; the only one that really matters. Some might play Manipulator as an influential Private Secretary, for example, operating beyond pubic view through carefully chosen puppets.

Those who enter the politics field in Altruist often find their avatar morphs: the system is enough to flip most players through Avoider into Cynic, as Dark State moulds them through deep-seated traditions and complex power games. Many entering government are first shocked by, but then gradually accept, the power that Dark Finance and Dark Corporation hold over government.

It's easy to acquire a sense of entitlement to the privileges of being at the centre of power. It's seductive to feel you can claim expenses for swimming pools and champagne. No wonder the rise of social concern in the politics field is alarming to the Dark Powers.

The Dark Powers are doing their best to get rid of checks and balances to government's power and decisions. They're even negotiating to scrap the Human Rights Act. This would legitimise Dark Media's 'national, racial or religious hatred that constitutes incitement to discrimination, hostility or violence' – although it already goes unchallenged by those administering the law of the land. Presumably, behind closed doors, many MPs are in Avoider: too afraid to challenge Dark Media for fear of being attacked. Others, playing Cynic, stand to gain.

Several Manipulator and Cynic MPs routinely avoid answering questions in parliament: either diverting the topic, or simply not showing up. Dark State say we have democracy, but players are misinformed and manipulated by Dark Media, and not taught at school to think for themselves. That's not democracy: that's downright dangerous.

In recent times, Dark State has grown increasingly confident about abandoning any pretence of democracy. They've tested the boundaries, and found they can get away with it. Thousands of players protested about badger culling, and hundreds of thousands protested about fracking, austerity measures and the government's refusal to take more refugees. But hundreds of thousands are not millions; Dark State has found they can safely ignore a huge mass marching for a day, or signing petitions.

Those working for Dark State use underhanded tactics to undermine opposition. Naturally, they vote against parliamentary reform and proportional representation. They maintain a two-party system, with all the Sleepwalking players all voting for them because they think there's no point in voting for anyone else. If the two main parties become corrupt, this is a real problem.

MPs for all major UK parties move into Avoider when a vote is called. Their conscience may tell them to vote for Life, but their party whip – their *whip*, let that sink in – instructs them by smartphone to vote the other way. They don't rebel too often in case it damages their career.

Behind-the-scenes Manipulators arrange cockfights between politicians. They orchestrate Dark Media smear campaigns, have opponents put under surveillance, or employ undercover agents to behave badly, masquerading as the opponent's supporters. Some play Cynic as paid consultant for political campaigns, advising on how to influence players' thinking without them knowing, or how to bias political TV interviews through clever camera angles, and psychologically undermine the guest the producer wants to take down.

Some MPs take 'cash for access' in parliament, and have relatives whose business influence reaches deep into policy making. Some have mutually beneficial relationships with Russian oligarchs, making it possible for elite criminals to hide their assets. At the hard end of the Cynic avatar are hitmen, contracted to take out key figures of political opposition. Morally, nothing is below them. Legally, they make sure they're covered.

Investigative journalist heroes expose lies and corruption in politics, but their role is becoming redundant. The Dark Powers have successfully created a culture in which truth and integrity no longer matter: lies and corruption are the norm; to be expected. Fortunately there are journalists and readers who are still awake and aware, still fighting for Life.

Dark State pushes the myth of austerity as it has always done, while the rich get richer. Knowing most players won't or can't resist increasingly harsh measures, they demonise those already marginalised and unable to fight back. They say there's no money for the most vulnerable in society, even though they're prepared to spend billions on war, nuclear weapons and high speed railways: a simple case of prioritising damage and destruction above Life, for power and profit.

They let rich offshore friends avoid paying into society while profiting from it, when their income and inheritance taxes could lift the entire population out of poverty. In return Dark State accepts donations from Dark Finance and Dark Corporation, and encourages Dark Media to announce biased information disguised as truth, or to spread rhetoric that encourages players to vote from fear.

Some players act out the Manipulator avatar on borough, district, town or parish councils. They give themselves pay awards while cutting services, force through decisions without local consultation, or hold meetings behind closed doors. The Manipulator avatar takes great pleasure in out-manoeuvring the opposition: for them that's part of the pleasure, and the reason for being in 'public service'.

At a global level, the Manipulators running the world are not politicians. Corporations are transnational, and individual governments have lost control. The World Trade Organisation operates on a global scale (and, of course, has a good share of Manipulator avatars). The World Economic Forum is made up of some of the world's richest people. Their Global Redesign Initiative proposes an end to elected governments negotiating trade treaties. Instead, a self-selected group of 'stakeholders' will make decisions on the world's behalf. They, not governments, are shaping and controlling the Game. And they are untouchable.

Perhaps you're a soft Cynic who has never voted, and doesn't intend to, believing all politicians are corrupt. But while you withhold your vote, Dark State wins. Despite popular belief, there are a lot of players trying to score for Life in the Politics field – and they need all the support they can get.

HOW TO SCORE FOR LIFE

All players can score for Life in this field in some way: through being active, or simply by voting.

Perhaps you are one who's never voted. You might have made a conscious choice not to play this field at all, preferring to stay clear of its power games; scoring for Life in other fields, building a better society from the ground up. Dark State hopes you'll carry on ignoring them.

Or maybe you don't know much about the parties and their policies, and you can't see voting making any difference. You've never thought about which policies score for Life and which enable harm. Dark State likes it that way; you're letting them get on with it. But as you, and many other players, grow more aware in this field you begin to connect your experience with decisions made in places of power; policies that affect you directly every day.

You realise your non-voting allows Dark State to get into power – that they then pass laws that give power to Dark Corporation, letting them trash the planet, kill wild creatures and suck the souls out of players. Shaken awake by eruptions in the Politics field, you find your avatar morphing – or you actively pick a different one – and you begin scoring for Life in this vital field, starting by turning out to vote for whoever has more policies that prioritise Life over money.

Many players vote Conservative from the Traditionalist avatar, for values such as family, decency and respect, and preservation of rural beauty. 'Conservative' by definition suggests a reluctance to change; a desire to preserve tradition. But the party has moved far from its core values, and is dominated by corporate interests. You might equally be a Traditionalist on the left of politics: dismissing cross-party alliances, or any politician who represents only some of your personal views.

All politicians, from whichever party, who rebel against the Dark Powers are hugely strengthened these days by social media support. When you openly serve Life in the public arena, you meet so much opposition from Dark State, Dark Media and their loyal players across the Game (and even other players on the side of Life) you need courage, and all the collaboration you can get.

Playing the Avoider avatar, you're aware that politics is a divisive topic that could lead to anger, bitterness or shame for you or others. You don't want the discomfort, so you hold back, and politics becomes an elephant in the room – so huge that it's hard to see over or round. You wait to see what others are thinking, maybe asking their opinions before supporting politics for Life, in case that's counter-current in your group. But as divisions become more starkly obvious, you know you're eventually going to have declare – even if choosing politics for Life makes you unpopular with your peer group.

Playing Altruist, you keep an eye out for injustice, corruption, and destruction. You can score for Life by signing petitions or attending protest marches. You know a healthy economy depends on healthy people and planet, not the other way round. So you vote for leaders who have Life at the heart of their concerns, rather than power and profit. You could use social media to share examples of Dark Media's political bias and misinformation, countering them with an alternative view – in clear but respectful language.

The Politics field is full of local Heroes. In Frome, Peter Macfadyen was frustrated with bickering between town councillors of different parties. He co-founded a group of independents, who now make up the entire council. This enabled a culture of collaboration, empowerment and excitement, which led to getting things done and scoring for Life. His book *Flatpack Democracy* inspires other towns to follow Frome's lead.

You might get involved in your borough or parish, sharing responsibility for decisions that affect wellbeing on your patch. Or you take some responsibility for people and place by getting involved in the countless enterprises and social structures that are springing up *despite* national and local government, such as the Transition Network and the People's Republic – building new structures under the existing one, ready for the collapse of Dark State.

These are models that offer more healthy and fair ways of doing society that all players can begin right away; an opportunity to create a new version of the Game that renders the Dark Powers' structures redundant.

Heroes at Westminster know that power corrupts, so they work for governance that is collaborative and wise. Hero MPs devise and support policies for wellbeing, not only for people but the whole living world. Whatever their party, when they defy the whip to vote for Life, they're playing Hero.

One regular Hero in the field is the SNP's Mhairi Black, who entered parliament aged twenty-one, fully embodying the Hero avatar. She has gained a well-deserved reputation for 'speaking truth to power'. Caroline Lucas is the Green Party's only MP, and it takes courage to maintain her voice and integrity. Her book *Honourable Friends* exposes the farce of an outdated political system, and the corruption and machinations of Dark State. She lays out sensible and compassionate alternatives, and celebrates political Heroes – not just from her own party. She is almost universally liked and respected, despite her regular vociferous attacks on Dark State.

Jeremy Corbyn (whatever you think of him as a leader) certainly plays the Hero avatar. He stands calm and strong in his defence of Life, despite the floods of abuse and spiked curve balls thrown at him by players of all parties. Some on the side of Life have genuine reservations about his decisions, and some are simply suckered in by the clever and thorough hatchet job of Dark Media, who don't want a Labour leader prepared to stand up to the Dark Powers.

Make no mistake: politicians playing Hero are using every ounce of courage, skill and integrity they possess as they fight to protect all players, and all of Life, from the Dark Powers that dominate politics. *They're doing it to protect you,* whether or not you're fooled by the Dark Powers' rhetoric and give them your vote instead.

Nationally, politicians from several parties work for a Progressive Alliance, with the aims of policies for Life and a fairer voting system. Corbyn, with the biggest progressive party and therefore the most to lose, will be playing Hero if he ever agrees to this. He hasn't yet – but he must, if he is serious about winning back the politics field from the grip of the Dark Powers.

If you're not sure about your MP, you can look at their voting record on They Work for You. Another website called Vote for Policies helps players identify the party that best represents their values; very useful for anyone thinking of changing avatars in this field.

The US has been side-swiped by the rise of Dark State, with Trump as its front – but the response from Life in this field has been powerful. Elsewhere in the Game, someone did get to play Hero in a presidential role. It was José Mujica, former president of Uruguay. He gently but stubbornly refused to accept the capitalist model. He lived humbly, perplexed by a world that sees this as eccentric rather than a normal way of behaving. He left behind him a healthy economy and social stability, showing that another way of governance is possible. It's worth checking him out on YouTube.

Even heads of councils, government departments or even countries find themselves in Avoider, unable to enact Life-protecting policies because Dark State advisors outnumber and manipulate them. They don't have the courage to speak publicly about what's happening, persuaded that to do so would be political suicide.

We urgently need politicians worldwide to play Hero: to have the courage to admit that democracy has been bought by corrupt big business, and that in reality its Manipulators pull all the strings – and to stand up to them. Only then can we overturn Dark State, and build something more healthy. Until then, Politics won't save the Game: quite the opposite.

Remember: scoring for Life in any of the fields is a political act.

State of Play

In the UK, the Politics field is currently owned by the Dark Powers, so they can design the Game in a way that suits them. But with daily political plot twists nationally and globally, the whole field is potentially up for grabs. Political Heroes are constantly trying to change the rules and break the grip of the Dark Powers. How this will play out is anybody's guess.

Resources for Life

Book: *The Establishment, and how they get away with it,* Owen Jones
Book: *Flatpack Democracy,* Peter Macfayden
Book: *Honourable Friends?* Caroline Lucas
Film: *The Riot Club,* Lone Scherfig
YouTube: Proportional Representation - Make Every Vote Count
YouTube: JFK to 9/11 Everything is a Rich Man's Trick
Prostitutestate.co.uk
Huffingtonpost.co.uk/politics
Voteforpolicies.org.uk
Politics.co.uk
Electoral-reform.org.uk
Petitions.parliament.uk
Other petition sites: 38 degrees, Avaaz, care2 and many more
Theyworkforyou.com

Field 10: Community

Community is a network of give and take relationships. A community can be extended family, a group of families, a neighbourhood, or players connected on the ground or online through a shared cause or passion. It can include the whole human community, and as we are part of nature it overlaps with the Animals and Planet Earth fields too.

THE DARK POWERS

During the industrial revolution a couple of centuries ago, traditional community became fractured as players headed to cities for work, unwittingly laying the foundations for the isolated consumer society so many experience today. In some places (often the poorest) community remains strong. But in wealthier areas, most players have never experienced long-evolved community with its interwoven history – something that was a fundamental part of our humanity.

As players became more financially independent, they didn't have to look out for each other any more. This may or may not be an intended consequence, but it suits the Dark Powers. They profit from a culture of individuality and competition, and actively promote fear of others. There is, of course, a risk in blind trust. But, good relationships are founded on trust: when players trust each other they care for each other more, and tolerance is higher. Mutual support scores for Life: hostility scores for the Dark Powers.

During the 1980s Dark State, in the shape of Margaret Thatcher, blatantly pushed competition, selfishness and greed. Today, Dark Media divides players with spite. Dark Corporation steals community activities such as sport, music-making, house-building and food production, and sells them back to players. And Dark Finance creates gross inequality leading to resentment and division. As communities disperse and their institutions disappear, there is no longer a common moral framework to counter the Dark Powers.

Giant property companies market their developments as new communities, but squeeze as much income out of a site as they can: no shared space for community, but crammed-in 'executive homes' which few can afford. This leads to a society of housing haves and have nots. Artificially inflated prices have nothing to do with bricks and mortar, plumbing and labour. There is plenty of land in the UK, and plenty of people willing to work at building their own home. A small plot isn't much to ask. Yet the Dark Powers hold the resources and control the market.

Some play the Cynic avatar buying property in city sectors where prices are spiralling, or acquiring 'holiday cottages'. Locals (if there are any left) complain that houses are unaffordable for their children, forcing them to move away. The Cynic shrugs; that's life. But it's not. It's death for that community. Homes that were built by and for a close network of families become rentable units of real estate, with a prime location or an expensive view.

One strong and ancient symbol of community, skill and competition is sport. It brings immense pleasure to participants and spectators alike, as well as a living for many. But it's been hijacked, *because spectators spend*. Manipulators milk that primal sense of shared allegiance through ever more expensive strips, tickets, and players. They don't need to care about the local community; most football teams' local roots are long gone.

Those who play sport professionally are controlled by corporate sponsors paying vast sums to have logos displayed. Whilst people starve, or wait for life-saving operations, a footballer is raking in around £44,000 per week. Just the steering wheel for a Formula 1 car can cost £40,000. The money sloshing around in sports could probably fund a universal family planning service, rapid development of renewable energies, and a massive ocean clean-up. But we lap it up, so they keep it going.

Another community treasure is art. Not so long ago, players everywhere made art of all kinds for their own and each other's pleasure, creating and maintaining strong bonds across families and generations. But the Dark Powers treat art as something players *consume*.

The worst kind of parasitic agent seduces artists with the lure of wealth and fame, and then creams off the profits. Their contracts are exactly as greedy and tight as they can get away with. Approached by desperate hopefuls whose marketplace has been flooded and monopolised, the Cynic doesn't ask, "Is it beautiful? Is it truthful?" but "How many will it sell?" If an artist's work sells, the agent shifts into Manipulator: simulating charm, concern and admiration to keep them pumping out the goods.

Meanwhile, global community is torn apart by violence and conflict, as arms companies sell the means for peoples to destroy each other. Suffering and death are their profit. Representatives of Dark Corporation meet in secret with Dark State, leaving some players wondering just how necessary all these lucrative wars truly are.

Wars are generally between Manipulator avatars. But they use Cynics to execute their plans, Traditionalists who engage in war because 'it's the right thing to do', and Sleepwalkers as cannon fodder. Unsurprisingly, a lot wake up when the fighting starts. Soldier Daniel Crimmins wrote a moving and illuminating piece about Sleepwalking into war. It's worth a read. (If you go to war genuinely wanting to fight the Dark Powers, maybe you're in Altruist or Hero.)

Some players act the Cynic in undercover surveillance, winning the trust (and even love) of players, and then reporting their plans to fight for Life to the Dark Powers. Others are trolls, paid to stir up fear, hatred, or suspicion; although some do it just to vent their bitterness. Some abuse their position of fame or respect in the community for their own gain: maybe financial, maybe sexual.

Some play Cynic in this field operating lucrative cults of pseudo-spirituality, and many operate underground, co-ordinating criminal activity. Some play a smaller Manipulator avatar in local community: pushing others around, they get their own way. Willing and able to damage others with malicious gossip, they gain a reputation as someone it's not wise to cross – so they go unopposed.

Others play Traditionalist working for Dark State, withholding support from desperate players who can't jump through benefit hoops, as depicted so powerfully in Ken Loach's film *I, Daniel Blake*. You could be the one who inserts spikes in retail meccas so that homeless people don't spoil the shiny face of shopping. You're sorry but you're just doing your job, implementing a system decided by those higher up. (If you enjoy the sense of power in an otherwise disempowered life, you're playing Cynic. If you have sleepless nights because of bad karma but can't leave, you're in Avoider.)

Every single player would benefit from doing community in a way that scores for Life, and nearly every player (apart from the true psychopath) is capable of doing so.

HOW TO SCORE FOR LIFE

You're scoring for Life when you're aware of your neighbours, people around you in shops or on the pavement, strangers you pass on an isolated footpath. Two hundred years ago this would have been a given in the places where we lived and worked. Today, Sleepwalking players don't know they're missing out on a sense of connection; a vital part of humanity and essential to emotional wellbeing.

When you're playing Altruist, you're ready to trust. Strangers have always been viewed with caution, but in most cultures travellers were once welcomed anyway. Travel is how broader networks of community stayed connected: how goods were exchanged (now done for us by supermarkets and Amazon) and how songs and stories were passed on (now done for us by the media, and Amazon). Waking up, you reclaim your humanity, no longer needing to fill your hunger for connection by consuming what the Dark Powers sell you.

On the side of Life you greet strangers, and speak with them if they're willing to engage (and you're in the mood). You forge connections, promoting a sense of wellbeing that tends to ripple on, and practise 'random acts of kindness', spontaneously (and sometimes anonymously) helping other players in need.

You're in the Avoider avatar if you see a Player struggling with a heavy load and feel an instinctive urge to help – but instantly check your impulse. You don't know them; what will they think of being approached by a stranger? But choosing the Altruist avatar you overcome your hesitancy, freeing yourself from the paralysis of Avoider, and maybe find that it feels very good, much better – for both of you.

You see a Muslim woman being insulted as she does her shopping. In Traditionalist, you don't want to challenge the abusers and get called a 'snowflake' or 'do-gooder' (community-dividing language of Dark Powers). But if you want to score for Life, you no longer want to collude; you know a sympathetic smile isn't enough. You find the courage to intervene, even if that just means ignoring the abusers and offering friendship to the woman. You might feel shaken, but you out-manoeuvred the Dark Powers.

Some play Traditionalist in viewing players from another class, place or lifestyle with suspicion. You're loyal to those within your boundary, wherever you've chosen to draw it. But fearing the unknown, you harden your heart to those outside that boundary, and the Dark Powers score. You score for Life when your sense of community expands beyond your immediate family to include more players in your geographical or online world, or even to all of humanity. And if your awareness of other species is high, you'll recognise that all Life is part of one big living community. What helps another living being benefits Life and benefits every player. What harms another living being hurts Life and hurts every player.

The Traditionalist avatar can be very strong on community. Playing this avatar you might vigorously defend local traditions such as the monthly coffee morning or annual carnival, scoring for Life. However, you might also believe that groups like Occupy, working to reclaim community, are all anarchists. This avatar respects authority – an attitude that only scores for Life when the authority figure is a community leader of wisdom and integrity, known to you and deserving of your respect. The Traditionalist also law-abiding – which is only appropriate when laws are designed to score for Life, and updated regularly to respond to an evolving Game. Plenty of murderous regimes have come about because players persisted in their trust of authority.

Playing the Altruist in community, co-operation is the natural state. You score for Life by supporting and enacting equality and respect for all. You avoid the Dark Powers' trap of turning different groups (such as gender, race or religion) against one another, causing further division. You look out for each other, and work together for the benefit of the group.

Perhaps you organise community activities. Or you do it less formally: for example, cooking and eating with others, sharing garden space with people who like to grow things, making music together and maybe dancing. Physical contact is important for psychological health in all primates, both in infancy and adulthood. Playing Altruist, you reject Dark Media's portrayal of physical contact as either violent or over-sexualised. You might bring safe and appropriate touch into your interactions, such as hugs: demonstrably good for wellbeing and bonding. When conflict arises (as it is bound to do), you and the community put time and skill into addressing and resolving it.

If you have a preference for your own space, that doesn't mean you can't play Altruist in community. You engage at whatever level feels personally right: with the right people, in the right way, for the right amount of time. It all scores for Life because there is strength in connection; divided and isolated players are easy prey.

Maybe you work in a community role, such as postman. Since the service was privatised your job is all about targets and efficiency, and no longer feels like a service. Some colleagues just want to get round as fast as they can and finish. But you're scoring for Life when you check on elderly players whose curtains are still drawn, or you agree to collect a prescription for a new mother – not because it's in your job description, but because you care.

Remember the saying that it takes a whole village to raise a child? This natural tendency is denied in a society where players are segregated into family units and age bands at school. Playing Altruist, you encourage players of all ages and genders to mix. Bullying and isolation become rare as young children learn from older ones, and older children naturally take a nurturing role with younger ones – whilst learning care and responsibility. Elders play an important role too: their stories and accumulated community wisdom are highly valued.

You might play the Hero avatar scoring for Life in your city, town, village or global community, working tirelessly for what you believe to be right: from gender issues to library provision; road maintenance to spiritual growth. Maybe you carry out and encourage acts of 'civil disobedience' in response to unjust and damaging actions of Dark State, risking arrest and imprisonment.

In inner cities, youth workers spend long hours trying to break the violent cycle of street gangs in which stabbings are commonplace. In rural areas, Heroes run campaigns to protect residents and wildlife from insensitive developments, and lead on Neighbourhood Plans that will help communities take back some responsibility.

Playing Hero in the global community, you see that Dark State is doing little to help players fleeing from war and climate change perpetuated by the Dark Powers. You take aid to Calais or other refugee camps – knowing that Dark State is detaining humanitarian Heroes under law supposedly designed for terrorists. The Transition Network, begun in 2007 by Rob Hopkins and Naresh Giangrande, plays international collective Hero. All over the world, Transition projects use a flexible framework to develop resilient local communities, each model appropriate to its context and culture.

In Bhutan, the Gross National Happiness project plays collective Hero in its experiment to design a society where happiness, not GDP, is the measure of success. Their work informs and inspires the global community to prioritise wellbeing above profit. In nearby Ladakh, Helena Norberg-Hodge charted the disappearance of community as the Dark Powers encroached from the west. She is now a prominent activist championing localism worldwide.

Shami Chakrabarty, founder of Liberty, is a human rights lawyer who has been attacked and defamed several times by Dark Powers who would like to silence her challenges. When she was nominated for a peerage, Dark Media were quick to smear her. Amnesty International plays a role as global community Hero, fighting the Dark Powers for human rights despite constant death threats and intimidation.

Luckily there are lower risk ways of playing the Hero avatar in community. Throughout human history, art has been used as a way of expressing and portraying the archetypal struggle between Life and the Dark Powers. Some artists (like Banksie) play Hero by making daring, subversive pop-up art that exposes or highlights corruption or destruction. A group of activists went to jail for creating a molasses 'oil spill' at the Louvre to protest about its sponsorship from oil giant Total (although some argue that taking Dark Corporation's money for the arts scores for Life).

You might be an artist, writer or artisan with a powerful message to convey; a vital role to play in the broader community. Friends and family are fearful when they see what you've made; you catch their fear and want to hide your work away. Or maybe your agent, playing Cynic, wants you to be more conventional, more commercial. You feel pressured to tone your work down. But you find the courage (maybe with the support of collaboration) to put it out there anyway; this piece of work you feel instinctively will score for Life.

Poets and storytellers often play Hero in community. They rap furiously like Kate Tempest, or write funny, gentle verse that demonstrates the unwitting absurdity of the Dark Powers, like Matt Harvey. Mythologist Martin Shaw plays Hero by keeping the ancient and vital art of storytelling alive and flourishing. Film maker Helen Iles used her inspiring film *Deep Listening* to explore the beauty and challenges of creating community in the 21st century.

When you buy mass-produced art you're making fat cats fatter, and skinny ones thinner. You're impoverishing the life of artists, and the life of Art itself – not least the precious dreams and visions that lie dormant within *you*. But when you reclaim music, reclaim art; create, commission, enjoy, share, you're scoring for Life – and enjoying yourself at the same time.

State of Play
Community is a field that's suffered severe losses to Life. The Dark Powers all but destroyed community as we'd known it from pre-history. Whether this was intentional or collateral damage is debatable –probably both. But though we can never recreate the intricate networks of people and place that evolved over thousands of years, players everywhere are creating strong new communities on their patch or online.

Resources for Life

Book: *Ancient Futures*, Helena Norberg Hodge
Book: *The Power of Just Doing Stuff*, Rob Hopkins
Book: *The Transition Handbook:* Rob Hopkins
Film: *The Economics of Happiness,* Helena Norberg Hodge
Film: *Deep Listening,* Helen Iles
Film: *I, Daniel Blake,* Ken Loach
Networkofwellbeing.org
Transitionnetwork.org
REconomy.org
Lammas.org.uk
Grossnationalhappiness.com
Gnhcentrebhutan.org
Liberty-human-rights.org.uk
Amnesty.org.uk
Occupy.com

Field 11: Animals

This field covers all the fellow inhabitants of our planet; those who evolved before us and alongside us. Of course, we humans are animals. But this field is about all the others: those who live with us as companions, those we keep captive for commercial use such as food or entertainment, and those who live free in their natural environment.

THE DARK POWERS

The Dark Powers see living creatures not as moving, breathing beings with their own heartbeat, but either as a resource to be exploited, or simply collateral damage from their activities in the Game.

This is bad news for other species. In late 2016 the London Zoological Society and the World Wildlife Trust published stats showing that we've lost 58% of global wildlife populations since 1970, and that losses are increasing. Make no mistake: we are in the middle of a slow-motion sixth mass extinction. And it's gathering pace.

Exploitation also causes daily suffering to the species still with us: cosmetics that involve invasive and painful tests on living bodies; medical experiments on creatures who have no choice but to endure agony day after day; industrial deforestation that leaves animals standing dazed and bewildered in a completely barren landscape that was their green and fertile home, buzzing with life. Then there is mineral extraction that poisons soil and waterways, choking the life out of billions of beings; the manufacture of household or industrial chemicals that wipe out fish and amphibians… it feels too much. It *is* too much.

The Manipulator avatar generally enjoys a luxurious life, untroubled by the suffering that feeds it. It has no compassion or respect for other living beings. Such assured arrogance blinds it to the fact that all humans are totally dependent on a healthy, biodiverse global ecosystem. Despite its cleverness, it doesn't realise it's destroying that which keeps us all alive.

Scoring for the Dark Powers in this field are the shadowy avatars who mastermind trade in rhino horns, or stage 'trophy hunting' for wealthy clients who feel good when they kill a big and powerful animal. They even make it a *cause célèbre*, like selfie-taking hunter Anna-Marie van der Westhuizen.

Elsewhere in this field, there's big money in the mega-dairy industry. Most operators (they can't be called farmers) are ruthless about their business: making cows' breast milk a cheap commodity whilst ripping day-old calves from their permanently incarcerated mother's udder, and shooting the males.

Factory farming Cynics rely on players being in Sleepwalker (or at least Avoider) to buy their goods. They know that most players, if they knew what happens behind the scenes, wouldn't dream of buying their meat or dairy products. So they hide the truth. Buildings are anonymous: no proud sign at the gateway. Unmarked lorries carry daily consignments of frightened animals along our roads and motorways to the slaughterhouse, or their corpses from slaughterhouse to factory.

Ads selling factory-farmed meat don't portray reality. Instead, they show a logo of a beaming pig wearing a butcher's apron and eagerly proffering a sausage on a fork. A lot of thinking went into this image. Marketers want players to associate their product with a children's story book pig, so that sausages seem benign and wholesome, rather than ground-up waste product from an incarcerated sow. And they get away with it. It's what players in Sleepwalker would rather believe, and it helps soothe the conscience of those in Avoider.

Cynic avatars might run a puppy farm, own a racehorse or operate an animal theme park for profit rather than vocation. The Cynic cares only about the physical wellbeing of the animals who earn them a living. Those animals' emotional wellbeing is of no interest (unless they become psychotic, unable to endure the stress of confinement – then they are no longer any use).

Some play the Cynic breeding, exporting or importing animals whose market price is high. Some deliberately breed designer dogs with such exaggerated features that they suffer, such as bulldogs with breathing problems. Those playing Traditionalist support tail-docking in terriers, and breeding boxers with hips so narrow it's almost impossible to give birth: the official 'breed standard' is sacrosanct.

Playing Traditionalist in this field, your beliefs about humans' place in the world are fixed and clear. Maybe you see suggestions that we're part of the animal kingdom as ludicrous. You can't say exactly why we're different – but you shouldn't need to. You think it should be obvious.

But any player can develop the awareness that in some ways we are much more like other living beings than we thought, and that those who are very different from us also appreciate freedom and wellbeing, and deserve as much respect. We are almost all capable of opening our hearts to the empathy that goes with that realisation. Once that happens, scoring for Life in this field becomes as natural as breathing.

HOW TO SCORE FOR LIFE

There is plenty of good news in the Animals field: some species are doing very well. As just one example: otters, back from the brink of extinction, are reappearing in England's rivers since clean water legislation came in and hunting was banned. More and more players are recognising that animals are of course sentient beings, and that harming them also harms the broader ecosystem.

When you're awake in this field you recognise that animals other than us also have hopes and fears; also experience joy, terror, boredom, discomfort or excitement. You know they have complex social lives, and are generally better at making simple decisions than we are. You no longer subconsciously think of them as cute animated toys, there for your enjoyment.

More and more studies are declaring various insects, mammals and even insects to be 'intelligent'; science is finally catching up with what humans always knew, until around ten thousand years ago. Never mind whether certain animals are almost as intelligent as humans: obviously, *all* have their specialities; things they can do better than us.

You might have believed humans were different from (superior to, dare we say?) other animals, and that made it alright to shoot geese arriving on the east coast of Scotland, exhausted by a long and difficult migration. Like Sir Peter Scott, you realise the paradox of your approach: you love wildlife and being in the countryside, so why kill the wildlife and support industries that destroy the countryside? You realise how absurd it is to 'do battle with nature', in your garden and elsewhere.

With your eyes open, you realise that animals aren't there to conform to your expectations. If your dog leaps into a muddy stream you might appreciate that he's hot, or thirsty, rather than *naughty*. He might not understand muddy cars, but he knows about regulating his body's temperature. You learn to gain respect, rather than exerting control or even violence to get the behaviours you want. You're playing Altruist when your interactions with other animals aim for *mutual* respect.

You benefit Life when you see pets not as possessions, but companions with their own preferences. Just as you might with other humans, you try to recognise when to touch an animal, and when to give him or her space.

Spending time with other creatures, getting close to them, you enter their world; whether physically or with a little imagination. You realise how your horse suffers with no shade or company in his grazing strip. You become aware that your dog, who you like to take everywhere, might actually have a preference for peace and quiet.

You can also score for Life by engaging your inner Cynic, realising you don't have to buy what Dark Corporation pushes for profit from animal-loving: manufactured toys, endless supplements and toiletries, and a whole wardrobe of clothes and accessories for animals. You discriminate between what genuinely keeps them well and happy, and what keeps you up with fashion but damages Life.

Many play Altruist in the Animal field, but are in Sleepwalker (or maybe Avoider) when it comes to pet food, for example, forgetting about the methane produced by animals farmed for cat or dog meat. Also, chicken meat for cats and dogs is generally factory-farmed. Sometimes it's a conscious choice as "it's only for the dog", but more often it's because pet food origins are seldom talked about and so not on most players' radar, even if they really care about the suffering of intensively farmed chickens. Once you know, it's up to you to choose.

Playing the Altruist avatar, you think about the impact your life has on other beings: the food you eat, the clothes you wear, the car you drive, the make-up you use, the stuff you buy – all have an effect on the wellbeing and survival of other creatures, other species and whole ecosystems. You realise that by making these choices with eyes open, you can reduce (if not eradicate) the impact of your life on other animals, and can sometimes actively help them.

Maybe you see the bodies of dead animals on the road, and you inwardly wince. Perhaps you feel bad that roads and motorways have made movement and migration dangerous or even impossible. You drive carefully so as not to accidentally take the life of a naïve young rabbit, an elderly pigeon or a fox with cubs waiting. Once, you would never have said this to anyone for fear of sounding eccentric or 'fluffy', but now you do – and find that people you might not have expected to, agree. As you move publicly into the Altruist avatar, they feel they can too.

You might realise you were playing Sleepwalker when, without really thinking why, you killed little creatures who appeared in your home. Playing Altruist, you ask yourself whether they'd do any harm living alongside you (some obviously would, but many wouldn't). You learn how much wildlife has been lost from the UK in the last hundred years. On a summer day you marvel at a butterfly-rich hedgerow, and realise *this is how it's meant to be* – this is how it was, until we killed most of our wildflowers for monocrop agriculture, and sprayed them with insecticides so a growing (and Sleepwalking) population could eat 'perfect' veg.

In your garden you can let Life flourish; let nature do its thing. It will soon visited by unexpected guests: bees, butterflies, and beautiful little winged creatures you never knew existed; slow worms, hedgehogs and even mammals. When you play Altruist, a surprising variety of fascinating creatures turn up and raise their families in the quiet, untidy corners of your garden (and your home, if you're willing!)

On holiday, you might see a horse taking tourists for rides in a carriage. It's pathetically skinny and has flies settling on its sore mouth, and a raw place where its harness has been rubbing. Naturally compassionate, you're upset. Defending Life, you can't keep quiet. Moving out of Avoider, you speak gently with the owner (who looks like he can't afford a vet). Fear of angering or humiliating him is overridden by your distress that the horse is suffering, and will suffer tomorrow, and the day after. And if you embarrass the people you're with, or spoil the experience for the kids – well, maybe next time they witness suffering, they too will have the courage to score for Life.

Imagine this: you see people on a beach passing round a stranded turtle, streaming themselves on Periscope. You're playing Avoider if you're shocked, but too paralysed to act. Maybe you even join in, though you're deeply conflicted: everyone else seems to think it's okay. But suddenly you know deeply that it isn't okay at all. You intervene on behalf of the turtle – and suddenly at least half the others, who felt the same way, are supporting you.

Maybe you take part in #MeatFreeMonday or #Veganuary. Out celebrating at a new restaurant, the chicken on the menu looks nice. For a moment you're tempted, but then you remember: this is the probably the breast of a broiler who's probably spent her six-week life crammed in an ammonia-filled shed, pumped with vaccines and developing sore feet as others die around her. So you ask if the chicken is free range, and your choice depends on the reply.

On Facebook you accidentally see an image of a factory-farmed pig being kicked in the face. You think: 'I'll never eat factory-farmed meat again,' and you really mean it. In the supermarket, though, you see the price of free range sausages, and reach out for your usual brand. But the image of the flinching pig's shocked face appears before you, and you spend a few extra pence on sausages from outdoor reared pigs.

To score for Life, you might avoid fish completely because of the immense pressures on ocean ecosystems. If you do eat fish, it's a small species from the bottom of the food chain, and you know for sure it's been sustainably caught.

You might choose to play Altruist by being completely vegetarian or vegan. However, you might also be a deeply committed vegan totally closed to the idea that any form of meat-eating might ever be alright for anyone, scoring for the Dark Powers as you rage at others.

To score for Life in this field you eat organic if and when you can, not only because it's good for your body, but to support soil improvement and reduce the spraying of poisons. This helps insects and other creepy crawlies survive, which in turn helps bigger creatures of all kinds.

You might work for one of thousands of charities, dedicating your life to the animal or eco-system you most cherish, or see as in most danger. Or maybe you support those charities in other ways: donating, signing

136

petitions, sharing posts on social media encouraging other players to score for Life in the animal field.

Playing Hero, you defend other creatures from the most destructive animal on Earth: the Human. Some play Hero on the ground: risking their lives to protect wild animals from poaching, trophy hunting or the destruction of their homes for logging, palm oil or peanuts. Some give up careers and dedicate their whole lives to running sanctuaries for animal victims of destruction. Collective Heroes include Sea Shepherd and Greenpeace, who among other organisations work in tough and dangerous conditions to defend marine life.

Author Jonathan Safran Foer went undercover to expose the sadistic horrors of factory farming in his powerful book *Eating Animals*. It was a hideous experience, but helped him score massively for Life. Advertising executive Kate Cooper stepped into Hero and made a film called *The Secrets of Food Marketing*: a film with a twist likely to get her booted out of lucrative Dark Corporation forever.

When the Dark Powers are publicly challenged, they move swiftly. Chris Packham played Hero when he wrote a column about the dangerous aspects of killing wild birds and animals for sport. The powerful Countryside Alliance quickly branded him an 'extremist', and asked the BBC to sack him. Social media made it possible for players everywhere to go to his (and Life's) defence.

Sometimes we need Heroes with courage to say the tough things, especially in a field where players want things to be nice. Facebook page *CCTV for all Slaughterhouses* posts horrifying images of cruelty. It alienates many with its relentlessly shocking images and severely-worded zero-tolerance for meat-eating. But for some, it's exactly what they needed to wake up to farm animals' reality. In all the fields, it takes courage to shake those who are asleep, and to risk losing loved friends and family in doing so.

Anyone can play Hero this field. Abuse of animals – whether wild, domestic or commercially kept – is so widespread that sadly, the opportunities are endless. You might start petitions about animal testing, bull-fighting, feathers ripped from live geese for pillows, mistreatment of circus elephants... sometimes feeling the sheer amount of diverse suffering could overwhelm you. But someone has to do this work, so you play Hero for as long as you can manage.

You might volunteer to help endangered species on the ground. Or you could challenge others who treat animals in their care badly; or question caterers or retailers about welfare standards of their animal products (if they don't know the answer, that tells you everything you need to know). Whenever you defend creatures who can't defend themselves, you're playing the Hero avatar.

State of Play

Life has taken massive, possibly fatal, hits in this field: suffering on an unimaginable scale, and an increasingly fragile complex network of Life. The good news is: most players don't want to hurt animals. Many are passionate about their wellbeing. Theoretically, Life should be in the lead in this field. It just needs more players to wake up to what's happening to animals, or move out of Avoider and make different choices.

Resources for Life

Film: *Cowspiracy,* Kip Andersen
Film: *Pig Business,* Tracy Worcester
TV: Springwatch, Autumnwatch, Natural World
Hashtags: #meatfreemonday, #veganuary
YouTube: How Wolves Change Rivers
YouTube: The Secrets of Food Marketing, Kate Cooper
Farmsnotfactories.org
Nonhumanrightsproject.org
Ciwf.org (factory farmed animals)
Rspb.org (birds and more)
Wdcs.org (whales and dolphins)

Thebrooke.org (working horses, donkeys and mules)

Rspca.org (domestic animal health)

Wildlifetrusts.org (UK wild animals by county)

Field 12: Planet Earth

Chilean poet Pablo Neruda wrote, "You can cut all the flowers but you cannot keep spring from coming." Yet we have seen the first signs of a disappearing spring. As the climate changes, weather is less stable, seasons less distinct. Add depleted, polluted land and a warming, acidic ocean: our planet is in crisis. A declaration of hope for today might be: "You can stop spring from coming, but you cannot stop Life on Earth from thriving."

THE DARK POWERS

The Dark Powers are destroying our precious world. Every day, careless industry adds to a devastating list: deforestation, soil depletion, dwindling and dirty rivers, toxic lakes, air pollution, plastic-filled seas, polar ice melt, acidified oceans and an increasingly unstable weather system. If you're not devastated by this list, maybe you're in Sleepwalker.

Manipulators instruct players to blow up mountains for the minerals inside, pollute waterways making them undrinkable and killing everything that lives in them, and pour toxic waste into the ocean destroying marine ecosystems. They order destruction of forests that are not only home to myriad creatures, but absorb carbon and exhale oxygen: the lungs of the Earth. Wild places are gouged out, and disappear under concrete.

To the Dark Powers, the Earth represents opportunities for speculation, acquisition and exploitation. To oil companies, the pure and beautiful Arctic is nothing but a vast oil well. To major housing developers, a wildlife-rich meadow is to be measured to squeeze in houses to a standard formula of space and profit. To global food producers, richly biodiverse habitat in Poland represents a new opportunity to grow cheap crops using insect-killing pesticides, flower-killing herbicides and chemicals that degrade the soil.

China has become the world's factory, and those who stand to profit care nothing for a population choking on air pollution. Dark Corporation rules a puppet government there, too. The Minister for Environmental Protection has acknowledged the existence of 'cancer towns' along rivers lined with factories – but has done little to address the situation.

Big players like the Koch brothers, who own the world's giant oil companies, pour vast funds into misinformation and propaganda, spreading confusion and doubt about whether climate change is actually happening – even as Arctic sea ice melts before our eyes. Sleepwalkers and Traditionalists are still buying the lie; the propaganda machine has some very credible people on its payroll.

Cuadrilla has permission from Dark State to ruin land and waterways though fracking as well as adding to carbon emissions. Fossil fuel manipulators schmooze politicians for tax breaks, and Dark State stifles and cripples competition from clean energy initiatives, through strict planning regulations and withdrawal of financial help. While the rest of the world moves ahead into developing renewables, the UK sinks back into fossil fuel dependency. Meanwhile, countries that have contributed least to climate change are the first to suffer.

Dark State attends climate talks and says all the right things, even claiming to lead the world on measures to halt climate change. Dark Media feed their hypocritical words to Sleepwalkers, who feel reassured. Then Dark State players go home and carry on dismantling clean energy initiatives, continue their support of oil companies and fracking, and plan to expand airports.

Playing soft Cynic, you might switch energy supplier to get the best deals, never mind whether the energy is renewable or burns fossil fuels. What's the point? You could be dead before the crap hits the fan. Disillusioned and bitter, you go somewhere beautiful – perhaps a park – to ease your soul. But you leave sweet wrappers on the grass, cigarette packets in the bracken, beer cans floating on the lake.

The Dark Powers destroy wild habitats to create cotton fields and peanut plantations. Cynics fell trees for wood products such as decking and furniture, and to clear land for beef and dairy cattle, creating a protein-rich diet that the world doesn't need. They destroy forests for palm oil to use in toothpaste, detergents, and shampoo. More forest is cleared every year – despite organisations like the World Resource Institute, Global Forest Watch and Greenpeace defending them. There are even plans to tear up rich and complex marine environments to get at gold beneath the sea.

In the UK, Dark State has stopped tree-planting subsidies, although trees score for Life in multiple ways: reducing flooding, hosting ecosystems, fixing soil erosion, providing renewable, non-toxic building material and absorbing carbon dioxide. Regardless of the science, most players know in their souls that trees are important; are practically sacred. Our instinct about trees is well founded: 'tree-hugger' is one of the most misguided of the Dark Powers' insults (as well as being shallow and meaningless).

But there are now payments for clearing 'unwanted vegetation' from 'productive land', so players in Cynic rip out ancient hedgerows and chop down mature trees that were not only thriving ecosystems, but were also helping prevent flooding. Land with the most desirable beauty: the peaceful estuaries, ancient forest, spacious moorland and wild coastline that we treasure for their soul-nourishing qualities – is bought up by the wealthy and powerful, jealously fenced off and forbidden to others, who accept the notion of 'trespassing'.

Those playing Manipulator and hard Cynic avatars see the planet's life support systems collapsing, and decide that if they're going to go down, they might as well go down rich. Using others as workers and consumers, they are like a virus or parasite. They are literally trashing the planet, lying skilfully to keep players not only ignorant but *helping*, totally unaware of the desperate battle Heroes are engaged in for the sake of all Life on Earth. Their greed will ultimately kill the host: a unique world, capable of supporting human life.

But those powerful Manipulators could realise that rainforests are worth more alive than dead, and that a dead planet is no good to them either. They could use their power, influence and intelligence to turn the Game around. They could easily wake up a whole world of players and lead them into scoring for Life on Earth, halting the damage, and aiding the creation of a healthy future on our Planet.

HOW TO SCORE FOR LIFE

If you've slipped into the Sleepwalker avatar in this field, there's a good chance you haven't spent much time in nature lately. Maybe you'd forgotten how nourishing, peaceful and inspiring wild places can be. Maybe it's even something you'd never experienced in your life.

If you want to score for Life, you might begin by going to beautiful places that nourish your soul and remind you of what really matters. Here, you rediscover the deep connection with your planet home that was always at your core, sleeping. Now you know what you've been missing; what you were *truly* hungry for. Getting to know the land in all its colours, contours, textures, and smells, you're somewhere on a journey of coming to love it deeply. Maybe you feel a special connection to forest, or mountains, or the ocean and its myriad extraordinary beings.

Or perhaps you're a pragmatist who is willing to score for Life on Earth, solely because you know we can't live without it. Your score counts just as much as any other Player's.

Coming out of Sleepwalker, you learn about the complex relationships between ocean and land, that forests are alive with communication through roots and fungal networks, that some bacteria can form rain clouds, and that whales play a role in carbon storage. You never knew the planet was so awesome! Now you see it is actually one giant living ecosystem, all its life interconnected and interdependent. It's obvious that damaging any aspect of the planet imperils the whole of Life.

Recognising Life as a vast, complex, fragile network of living beings, soil and rock, water and air, and you take your unique role in it seriously: acting in ways that defend and benefit the greater living good. You use your work, your purchasing choices, your interactions and your vote to score for Planet Earth. You think about your children, and their children, and live in ways that ensure the best possible Life for them and all the creatures they'll share the world with.

You encourage your children to make dens, pick up pine cones and lie on their backs in the grass watching clouds. For city kids, a park may be the only chance they get to experience the natural world. Parks provide players of all ages with their only lifeline of calm, nourishment and connection with what really matters. And yet Dark State is selling parks off as 'expendable'.

If you've been playing the Traditionalist avatar, you probably didn't believe climate change was happening. As if we could affect the weather! A bit of heavy rain, and everyone starts jumping up and down predicting imminent doom. But as the majority view becomes apparent, you accept that weather patterns are changing because of rapidly increasing carbon dioxide in the atmosphere. Then maybe you throw all your weight into defending the magnificent tradition of Life on Earth.

If you've been playing the Avoider avatar you probably knew, deep down, that the scientists were right. Maybe you even had nightmares about it, but put off doing anything – hoping the science was overly pessimistic, or that some techno-fix would stabilise the climate. Maybe you thought you couldn't do much anyway: runaway climate change is the most overwhelming scenario you could imagine.

Reading that it's not too late to act, you think about getting solar panels, and discuss it with your friends. You debate feed-in tariffs and payback times and then, somewhat embarrassed, admit also wanting to cut carbon emissions. But you discover that everyone else has the same unvoiced concerns. In this field you are not alone: there are countless players in Avoider (although you can't see they are, as they can't see you are).

Selecting the Altruist avatar, you keep your impact on living systems as low as possible. You find alternatives to plastic products like cotton buds, razors, cups, bottles and pens. You keep a low carbon footprint by buying less stuff, using less energy, cutting down on driving and flights, switching your engine off, switching to ethical energy companies, generating your own or community energy, growing and making your own, or buying locally made.

You support Heroes in their planet-protecting work by signing petitions, joining marches, voting, giving to charities, sharing information, giving to crowdfunding, going to meetings and rallies, or whatever way works best for you.

Playing Altruist, you naturally take personal responsibility for whatever little patch of the planet you're on: for example picking up plastic from the street, or the beach. You know that methane from farmed animals is a major greenhouse gas, so you cut down, or cut out, meat and dairy. You realise it's not possible for anyone to play Altruist 24/7 and you don't give yourself a hard time for that; you just do what you can, when you can. You're kind to yourself as well as other players and non-human life.

In this sad stage of the Game where greed and cruelty are portrayed as the norm, others might call you eccentric for protecting what is not only a beautiful planet, but the only home we have. But the Dark Powers make 'environmentalism' seem like a hobby of choice, rather than a time-consuming and sometimes distressing commitment to defending Life on Earth from destruction. Maybe you respond by playing Hero and taking some form of leadership role: challenging the Dark Powers, and encouraging other players to score for Life.

Two players who've taken risks in founding ethical energy companies in the UK are Dale Vince of Ecotricity and Julia Davenport of Good Energy. They've developed successful businesses and clean energy supplies, despite Dark State moving to block their innovations and Dark Media almost completely ignoring what they're doing. But playing the Hero avatar they are courageous and resourceful, and won't be thwarted.

As fast as fracking opens up a new seam of exploitation, Hero avatars are on the case. A group of protesters at a test site near Balcombe were arrested, which gave a clear message to those who would stand in the way of Dark State and Dark Corporation. But Tina Louise Rothery and others continue to play Hero and hold the line against fracking.

Meanwhile, author and ecologist Glenn Edney plays his Hero avatar by dedicating his life to service of the ocean. His book *The Ocean is Alive* invites players to fall in love with ocean life, and the ocean herself. In this new magical relationship, you are inspired to score for Life in this vital realm rather than unwittingly serve the Dark Powers, harming what you love without even knowing.

The Rainforest Alliance defends the 'lungs of the Earth': the vital and precious biodiverse inhabitants of forests, and the livelihoods of players who live and work in them. And the World Land Trust protects species-rich and threatened habitats, acre by acre.

In the UK, the Eden Project is a visitor attraction showing examples of plant life across the world. Everything it does is with Life in mind and wellbeing as a goal. It attracts millions of visitors and so its score for Life is substantial. However, all of this biodiversity is contained within two domes and a bowl.

Writer and activist George Monbiot calls for 'rewilding': a restoration of the whole country's forest and wild animals, most of which have been wiped out by large scale, insensitive, unsustainable farming.

And because we still need to produce food, the Landworkers' Alliance helps people who make their livelihoods from the land, producing food, fuel and fibre using sustainable methods, and the Permaculture Association helps people 'design intelligent systems which meet human needs whilst enhancing biodiversity, reducing our impact on the planet, and creating a fairer world for us all.'

Joanna Macy is one of the true wise elders of the world. Most of her Life's work has been dedicated to what she and colleague David Korten call 'The Great Turning'. Her vision has long been a shift from the industrial growth society to a Life-sustaining civilisation. Her 'Work that Reconnects' encourages and inspires players in "this extraordinary time in human history when perceptions of reality are shifting, and human minds and hearts are opening to the fact that we are the world, and the world is us".

On the more practical side, Polly Higgins plays Hero in advocating for the criminal offence of Ecocide (extensive damage to, destruction of or loss of ecosystems). As she puts it, "Now I use my legal skills for just one client: the Earth." But the law is intended to protect all the inhabitants of the planetary ecosystem under threat of damage or destruction.

The entire living Earth is at risk of commercial exploitation as companies move to privatise rainwater. When this happened in Bolivia, the people fought back hard – and won. The land, the seas, and the air you fly through: all are claimed by someone. There are even discussions about ownership of the moon.

In 2016, Standing Rock became an iconic symbol of the Game, as Hero avatars fight desperately and bravely to protect their land from the planned giant oil pipeline. They were joined by brothers and sisters from across the continent and around the world: a momentous and significant struggle between Life and the Dark Powers.

Our planet needs all the Heroes it can get. Fortunately, it has some powerful ones, and more are stepping up every day.

State of Play

Planet Earth, our only home, is in crisis. Some scientists call this the Anthropocene Age: plastics, carbon emissions and nuclear explosions are beginning to show up in the geological history we're creating. If the Dark Powers win this field, all the other fields instantly become irrelevant. Hero avatars are fighting hard for Life on Earth, but can only succeed if enough players wake up and come together to halt the destruction.

Resources for Life

Book: *Animate Earth,* Stephan Harding

Book: *Rewilding,* George Monbiot

Book: *The Ocean is Alive,* Glenn Edney

Book: *The Great Turning,* David Korten and Joanna Macy

Film: *An Inconvenient Truth,* Al Gore

Film: *Gasland,* Josh Fox

Facebook: 350.org

Soilassociation.org

Rainforestfoundation.org

Foei.org (Friends of the Earth)

Greenpeace.org

Oceanspirit.org

Edenproject.com

Joannamacy.net

The Game: State of Play

"Life is to be lived, not controlled; and humanity is won by
continuing to play in face of certain defeat."— Ralph Ellison

THE GAME has recently moved to the next level – you can feel it. players everywhere are waking up. The Dark Powers are being unmasked, and creative responses for Life are springing up all over the world.

Altruist avatars multiply daily as players change careers, form off-grid communities, make their own music, or simply eat good food. New Heroes step forward, finding their unique voices. As tension heightens and players rally to either side, artists of all kinds, from Leonardo de Caprio to Lily Allen, publicly declare for Life. Grassroots movements are sprouting everywhere, creating thriving communities and healthy land around them. Life is reasserting itself, reaffirming itself, in myriad ways.

But in response to this positive surge of Life, hate movements proliferate and corporations' grip on the world tightens. Ethics are subverted: decadence is desirable, healthy is geeky, violence is cool. In the UK and the USA, Dark State control grows heavier, with more harsh and destructive measures announced every week. And across the world, survivors of destruction stand dazed and bleeding in the ruins, whether a small boy in a bombed city or a baby orang-utan in a bulldozed forest.

With fewer places to hide, The Dark Powers are being forced out of the shadows. As Manipulators become daily more blatant, players are awakening to the reality of the Game. Tension between the forces of Life and the Dark Powers is heightening fast, and it's hard to predict how it will play out – for people or for planet.

Science suggests that climate change is accelerating more rapidly than we thought. At Paris in 2016, world leaders agreed to aim for a limit of 1.5 degrees planetary warming. But despite good efforts from some countries, in a Trump-led world it's unlikely that many attempts will even be made, let alone successful ones. At four degrees there won't be a tree left standing, anywhere. On our current trajectory we're heading for six degrees, which is obviously Game Over.

Joanna Macy writes that the accelerating pace of destruction may already be taking us beyond tipping points where ecological and social systems unravel irreparably. Alongside the Great Turning, the Great Unravelling is happening too (if you want the science, check out Rockstrom's 'planetary boundaries').

Meanwhile, society unravels too. When the Pope delivered his Encyclical and the world didn't change overnight, the Dark Powers became more bold. The highest authority for Good had spoken, and seemed to have been ignored. Extreme leaders taking power around the world have incited and normalise prejudice and hatred. Individuals like Trump upturn moral norms like teenagers: pushing boundaries and getting away with it, and liking the sense of power. Friends, families and communities are pulled apart, no longer able to ignore each other's political views – or their implications. Gone is the commonly agreed social rule not to discuss politics: as players divide on fracking and renewables, Europe, immigration, strikes, nationalism, and political leadership, everyone's talking about it.

In the next phase of the Game, these splits won't be only political. They will increasingly be between self-interest and compassion. We're now confronted with the reality of the Dark Powers' assaults on Life; the growing corruption of politics, media, business and economics. We have to decide whether we're willing to compromise – to sell our souls – or not.

A whole lot of players are already shifting avatars, and further changes in the world will make tough choices inevitable. Will players suddenly flip into Altruist and Hero avatars because time is short? Will it be like the blitz, with everyone pulling together against a common threat? Or will there be blatant control, crime and cruelty as Cynics and Manipulators take off their masks? The answer is probably both. We already see some young people fully aware of the Dark Powers and ready to fight, and others completely sucked into the illusion, because they have never known anything else.

As the divide increases, those who usually play the middle three avatars will increasingly jump either way. Some will choose to act on behalf of Life: we'll see a flourishing of Altruist and Hero avatars in the world. Others will choose to play Cynic, abandoning hope and looking after themselves, like looters. Still others will play Manipulator and milk it for every last bit of profit, right up till the end. This scenario is already playing out in slow motion – and is set to speed up quite quickly.

Don't be misled: Manipulator avatars have the controls in this Game. Hero avatars are engaged in a perpetual battle: working to defeat the Dark Powers, to defend Life and to co-create a healthy reality for people and planet. Life isn't going to win this stage of the Game by outsmarting The Dark Powers, or by being more powerful, or even with that magic tool: love. Some of the most powerful Manipulators are clinical psychopaths, and can never respond to a light touch. Beyond the reach of compassion, they are the most dangerous players. Right now the Dark Powers look like winning hands down, *because most players are letting them*.

Cynics profit from destruction, Traditionalists defend systems riddled with corruption, and in Sleepwalker we have no idea all this is going on. In Avoider we know, but we do nothing. We're only supporting Heroes'

151

work when we play the Altruist avatar. So the only way Life can prevail is by players selecting Altruist or Hero. It's not about Life taking the Dark Powers' pieces off the board: it's about most of those pieces magically changing colour.

There is a flaw in the Dark Powers' strategy. They believe, and have us believe, that we depend on them. But actually it's the other way round: *they depend on us*. They rig the rules of the Game to suit them, but we don't have to accept those rules: we can create our own Game. It's very simple. The fewer players buy Dark Corporation's stuff, borrow Dark Finance's cash, accept Dark State's damage and swallow Dark Media's bile, the more they are reduced to the point of futility and lose their dominant role.

If we all continue playing by the Dark Powers' rigged rules, one obvious and imminent outcome is runaway climate change. But even then, it won't necessarily be Game Over for Life on Earth. If we go, (which we certainly will before we hit a six degree rise) we'll take most other species with us. But some creatures and plants will almost certainly survive, and new forms of life will evolve – just as they did after the other five mass extinctions. For them, the Game could go on for millions more years, until the sun cools down. We just won't be there to see it.

Great civilisations have arisen, and flourished, and fallen into decay plenty of times before. The damage of the decline phase has always been local and short-term, with a new civilisation always ready to emerge elsewhere. The difference in this Anthropocene Age is that such a decline will inevitably affect the whole world.

But there are plenty of alternative endings. Things can change quickly, although we never expect them to. Any number of events could bring our part in the Game to an end: a meteorite, nuclear war, a virus that wipes out humanity. A mini ice age could arrive. A super-volcano could erupt, taking humanity with it.

Would an imminent end to the Game for humanity make it not worth playing? Perhaps the exact opposite is true. If we knew a lethal super-volcano was going to erupt this century, that would be all the more reason to make our *now* as good as it can possibly be. The Dark Mountain project provides a community for those who agree that 'We live in a time of social, economic and ecological unravelling. All around us are signs that our whole way of living is already passing into history. We will face this reality honestly and learn how to live with it.'

The choices of each Player from this moment forwards will determine whether the Dark Powers win this phase of the Game, or whether humanity is able to mitigate and survive this current mass extinction. *If enough players choose Life, we could just emerge from this turbulent phase ready for a new beginning.* Even if we stop burning fossil fuels now, climate chaos will get worse for a while. Then it will begin to level out as a long, slow recovery begins. players in the Game at this time (which may well include you) will transition bumpily to a very different world, and will learn to adapt and collaborate. Depending how it's handled, this could be a time of great opportunity, creativity and fresh beginnings. The Pope's words were not in vain: they entered our consciousness, and played a part our waking.

Players who now choose to act for Life need to collaborate: not just in the future, but today. The future is in our hands, so it's essential that we build and maintain strong and supportive relationships. We all make mistakes, we are all fallible. But we can't afford to judge and criticise one another. Seriously: there isn't time for that. Instead we need to support anyone trying to score for Life, whatever shape it takes.

You might want to score for Life because you believe in a better tomorrow. Things don't look good but a plot twist is always possible, and it's vital that we play the Game with that in mind, and *as if it will happen.* Who knows what miraculous events might bring about a victory for Life: a tomorrow of freedom, peace and wellbeing.

But whatever the outcome, why would we even wait for a better tomorrow, when we can, in each moment, create a beautiful today?

Debrief

"You cannot get through a single day without having an impact on the world around you. What you do makes a difference, and you have to decide what kind of difference you want to make."

– Jane Goodall

In researching and writing this book I've felt disturbed, overwhelmed, disbelieving, hopeful, shocked, angry, defensive, and inspired. Maybe you've felt some of these while reading it, too.

I wanted to write a poetic, mythical book about light and dark in the world; something gentle but profound. But *The Game* is what came out. Three times I walked away from it – and three times it called me back. So I conceded that in these turbulent times, it must be needed. Anyway, there are already plenty of excellent poetic and mythical books on this topic; it seemed important to lay out in real terms the impact of what we all do on the ground, day to day, for better and worse.

When I shared the original idea with a potential editor he said, "You're trying to write the world, and that can't be done." Nevertheless, I felt compelled to make the attempt. The structure of avatars and fields helped me 'write the world' in a simple format. Reality is, of course, far more complex. To do such complexity justice would take a vast academic treatise, and that still wouldn't be enough. And at the rate the Game is accelerating, I had neither time nor desire to research and write such a book. There are also already plenty of well-researched volumes on the topics I've brought together. You can fact-check everything here if you want to.

The way the Game is moving, by the time you are reading this there will be new developments since I wrote it: positive initiatives from those fighting for Life, new manoeuvres from the Dark Powers, and new awareness of your own game-plan.

It's not my wish to criticise any individual player, although it may feel like I am. We are where we are, each of us, and like you I'm always learning; doing the best I can. But I *am* calling out the Dark Powers, and what they can do through any of us when we unwittingly allow them. I can't and won't stand by and simply let them quench Life, although my knowledge and skills (and courage) sometimes feel inadequate.

Players who have declared for Life often experience a form of 'humble Altruist', pointing out strenuously that it's not 'us and them'; that the Dark Powers are in all of us. Of course they're right. But in acknowledging that, it's vital that we also acknowledge another reality: some of us score more for the Dark Powers than for Life, and some score more for Life than the Dark Powers. This is not because the latter are intrinsically better people. It is for two very simple reasons: 1) they are aware of the danger Life is in, and 2) they choose to do something about it. Anyone is capable of both, and this book is to 1) state clearly the danger Life is in and 2) describe things people can do about it if they choose.

It's important to remember that no-one can play Altruist or Hero all the time – even though some players will expect you to. When you don't (which you won't, because you're human) some will be indignant, likely covering their disappointment at your fallibility. You're an unwelcome reminder that it's not possible to be perfect. And perhaps you also remind some players uncomfortably that just because you're not a perfect Hero, you don't have to just abandon the Game to Dark Powers. *Every* Player can do something, and it all helps. Holding an intention to score for Life more often will make a huge difference to your bit of the world.

Sometimes you'll do something you know scores for the Dark Powers, like taking a long-haul flight – or not do something for Life, like leaving that plastic bottle lying on the beach. You're not playing Cynic: you care. You're not in Traditionalist: you don't accept these behaviours as the norm. You're not Sleepwalking: you know the impact. And you're not in Avoider, because you don't give yourself a hard time. It could be said that you're in a place of 'resting Altruist'. Maybe you intuitively know that giving yourself permission to rest means you can be more effective at scoring for Life over the long Game. Life calls you urgently. But – unlike the Dark Powers – it doesn't seek to control you. Rather it seeks to free you from control.

Although I'm on the side of Life, inevitably I score for the Dark Powers sometimes, as does everyone. I can only describe the avatars *because I know them all from the inside* – except global Manipulator, for which (thankfully) I have neither the strategic , nor the ability to emotionally detach so completely.

This isn't a book about moral superiority. It's a book describing choices that support world wellbeing, and choices that enable destruction. But I can't avoid being subjective; as with any writer, my personal values obviously shape the worldview I present. I'm not asking you to share my values: only to take a part in maintaining the Life support systems of the planet on which we all depend.

A friend who read an early draft asked (with some trepidation), "What do you want this book to achieve – do you want everyone to become Heroes?" I said no. In the Game, nobody can 'become a Hero'. No-one fits neatly into just one avatar, or spends their whole life in just one. We all occupy different avatars in different fields, sometimes simultaneously.

Anyway, the Hero avatar is only needed in direct proportion to the threat Life is under from the Dark Powers. In my ideal outcome, most players have woken up, or freed themselves from the paralysis of Avoider. Everyone plays Altruist more often, scoring for Life through their work, purchases and activities, and we all enjoy a mostly peaceful, equal and healthy society and planet. Those who have been playing Hero can go home and have a cup of tea.

My dream is of a tipping point where it becomes *normal to live in ways that benefit Life*. In my vision,. People play Traditionalist by scoring for Life because it's the done thing. There's no-one in Sleepwalker, because everyone knows about the Game. There's no need to play Avoider, our fear of the Dark Powers has been justified, and our fear of social exclusion is redundant. Those playing Cynic play a healthy Cynic. Players can still make money and gain prestige, but they do it in sustainable, renewable ways. There are more players in Altruist every day, free now to just get on and do their thing, with no need to support Heroes in their work. (The Hero avatar is almost out of a job – but not quite. The Dark Powers may be diminished, but are never completely defeated.)

But my vision isn't the point. 'The Game' is not real; it's only my version. Your version is almost certainly different: shaped by your own passions, concerns, and beliefs. You might include fields I've barely touched on. You might see the avatars differently; perhaps you'd have a whole different set of avatars. Indeed, your version of the Game might look and feel totally different to mine.

One thing is true, though: whether you choose to play this version, your version or none at all, *you're still in the Game, right now*. No-one can opt out of scoring.

Day by day, moment by moment, we are all shaping the outcome – and we are all part of the outcome.

Your move.

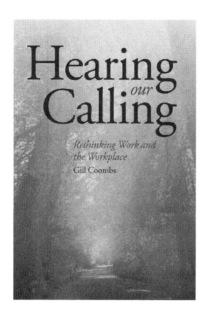

At its best, work can be a joyful, fulfilling activity that contributes something positive to the world. But most people today dislike their jobs, many suffer from work-related stress, and much human endeavour causes damage to society and our precious world.

Gill Coombs' book Hearing our Calling, published by Floris in 2014, looks at how this has happened, and suggests how we can each create a different reality for ourselves. Coombs believes we all have unique gifts, and can use them to create a positive future for people and planet – whilst loving what we do.

Praise for Hearing our Calling

'Hearing Our Calling is an important and valuable contribution to the work of re-visioning how we want to experience our western societies.' GLENN EDNEY, author of *The Ocean is Alive*.

'Hearing our Calling is an inspirational invitation to re-evaluate what is truly important and meaningful to us in our work.' SIMON ROBINSON, co-author, *Holonomics*.

Printed in Great Britain
by Amazon